Vineyard Confessions

TALES OF MENOPAUSE, LOVE AND NATURAL WINE

CARO FEELY

WWW.CAROFEELY.COM

Reviews of Caro Feely's books

Praise for Vineyard Confessions (previously Glass Half Full)

'Honest and touching.' Martin Walker, bestselling author

'Caro Feely is a force of nature! Caro draws the reader into her world with its all of its challenges, triumphs, and heartaches.' Mike Veseth, The Wine Economist

'Vineyard Confessions is a love story poured beautifully.' Robyn O'Brien, bestselling author

'A brave and compelling tale.' Alice Feiring, author and wine writer

Praise for Grape Expectations

'Captivating reading for anyone with dreams of living in rural France.' Destination France

'Really liked Caro's book! Definitely the best – and most realistic – tome coming from the 'A Year in Provence' genre.' Joe Duffy, Irish radio personality

'Bright, passionate, inspiring, informative and absolutely delicious' Breadcrumb Reads blog

'Filled with vivid descriptions of delicious wines, great food... a story of passion, dedication, and love' Bookalicious Travel Addict blog

Praise for Saving Our Skins

'Earnest and winning... sincere and passionate' Eric Asimov, New York Times

'So impassioned that it could inspire you to drop all security, move to the backwaters of France, and bet your life, all for the love of making wine.' Alice Feiring, author and wine writer

'Required reading for anyone who loves wine! Even a teetotaller will drink up every page for the fascinating behind-the-scenes of organic farming.' Kristin Espinasse, French Word a Day

'Caro has produced a beautifully written sequel which in turn seduced and terrified me about the prospect of owning an organic vineyard in rural France. I thoroughly enjoyed the urgency of her writing.' Samantha Brick, author and journalist

'Caro Feely understands that winemaking is an art, a science and a business. Saving Our Skins entertains and informs as it tells the story of her family making organic and biodynamic wine in the south of France. Required reading for wine lovers everywhere.' Mike Veseth, The Wine Economist

This is a story about the ebb and flow of life and love, of living and dying, a shout for the earth, for nature, for us and our future.

In memory of Peta-Lynne 'Blossom', our beloved Mum Feely

Also By Caro Feely

In the Vineyard Series:
Grape Expectations
Saving our Skins
Vineyard Confessions (previously titled 'Glass Half Full')
Cultivating Change

Prequel to the Vineyard Series:
Saving Sophia

Non-fiction
Wine, the Essential Guide

VINEYARD CONFESSIONS

This 2023 edition published by:

Caro Feely

www.carofeely.com

First published under the title 'Glass Half Full' by Summersdale Publishers Ltd, UK, in 2017

About Caro Feely

Caro traded in her life as an IT Strategy Consultant to pursue her dreams. She writes books and runs an organic estate with wine school, yoga school, and accommodation, in South-West France with her partner, Sean. She's an accredited wine educator, a registered yoga teacher, a confident and engaging speaker and an experienced virtual event facilitator. Follow Caro by joining her newsletter at www.carofeely.com and connecting at www.instagram.com/carofeely or via the social media network links below.

instagram.com/carofeely

facebook.com/caro.feely.wines/

linkedin.com/carow

amazon.com/author/carofeely

goodreads.com/author/show/6176029.Caro_Feely

Note from the Author

This book is memoir. It reflects my recollections of experiences over time. Some names and characteristics have been changed, some events have been compressed or changed, and dialogue has been recreated. Thank you for joining me on this journey.

Contents

The room went quiet for a moment. Outside, vine-covered hills ran into the distance, filling the panoramic windows. Inside, walls of limestone and a ceiling of poplar and oak enclosed the scene, the natural materials brought a sense of solidity and calm. But it was harvest, impossible to feel calm.

After spitting I looked up and saw a thunderhead in the distance. It spread like a charcoal-coloured duvet being shaken over the blue sky, then hung still for a few moments before growing and moving closer. Its dark grey curves plumped out.

'The taste is our *terroir*,' said Sean, seemingly oblivious to the storm cloud. 'With our natural farming, the wine reflects the limestone that underpins our vineyard; you taste the ancient seabed in the glass. If you lick the roof of your mouth you'll find a hint of salinity, like a sea breeze.'

'Hmm, yes, I see what you mean,' said Christophe.

Sean's description transported me back to a visit to a Loire Valley winegrower had sparked our dream to go wine-farming in France. We had planned and saved for almost a decade. After years of searching, we found our vineyard, the one we were looking on to. It had been in liquidation, a 'fire sale'. We told ourselves it had potential, but we had to look beyond the rotten shutters, un-trellised vineyards, rusted fences and mouse infestation. Sean returned from his fact-finding visit and said, 'It looks like the vineyards of the *premier grand cru classés* we visited in St-Émilion.'

We were idiots without a clue but, after tasting the wines and seeing the views, we were smitten, our rational selves swept away by an unaccountable force, a passion, a deep need to grow and make our own wine. We sold up, left our jobs and put everything into the failing farm. Since that shaky beginning, we had farmed organically and it showed. The Sauvignon Blanc was clean and carried notes of grapefruit, gooseberry, and lemon, on a cool undertow of limestone.

'We harvested the Sauvignon Blanc this morning,' said Sean.

'What was it like?' asked Christophe.

'Smooth,' replied Sean.

They were men of few words.

'It's rare for it to be smooth,' I added. 'Simple; yes. Smooth; no.'

They laughed.

'Every year we're guaranteed some breakdown and the expensive repairs that go with it,' I said.

'I know the feeling,' said Christophe, whose family owned a vineyard. 'It's a juggling act.'

I pushed the thought of machinery breakdown out of my mind and opened the *La Source* red, a classic St-Emilion-style blend of Merlot, Cabernet Franc, and Cabernet Sauvignon. As I poured, the room darkened, as if following the change in colour in the wines. We gathered closer to the windows, fascinated. The cloud mass grew, the initial dark bank expanding like a tidal wave rolling in slow motion across the sky. The room went dark as if night was falling. The top of the almond tree in front of the tasting room began to thrash, then the lower-level cherry trees and hazels followed. I felt a shiver of dread and saw a similar look on Sean's face.

The poplars on the driveway began to swirl like mops shaken by angry cleaners. A few large dark circles splatted on the terrace outside. I tried to calm myself. *It's OK –*

it's only rain. As if hearing my internal voice, the wind upped the ante, thrashing the trees more ferociously and making the vines on the hillside dance like dervishes. With each passing second the drama notched up like a Wagner symphony. The first hailstones clattered on the terrace, and I felt a bolt of adrenalin.

My attention was drawn to a car pulling in alongside the tasting room. Michael and Lisa, architect and artist from London, were regular guests to the Feely Wine Lodge. I waved from the window, not chancing going out into the violent weather. They waited a few minutes, hoping the storm would ease. It got worse. They threw caution to the wind and raced inside. We kissed hello and I introduced them to Christophe.

'I'd better get you over to the Lodge before it really comes down,' I said, taking the keys from the counter, delighted to have something to take my mind off the brewing disaster.

'What does this mean for the harvest?' shouted Michael as we stepped into the maelstrom. I could barely hear him above the noise of the storm.

'I don't know. We have to wait and see,' I yelled. 'Be careful you don't slip.'

In the few seconds crossing the uncovered section of timber deck from the tasting room to the Lodge we were soaked. I opened the door and hung on to it with all my strength to stop the wind giving it a life of its own.

'*Bonne installation!* Happy settling in. I'll be back with a gift bottle of wine when the storm eases. Cross your fingers that it isn't too destructive!' I shouted, laughed hysterically, then forced the door closed behind me, it took all my power to keep control of it against the strength of the wind.

A pile of hail had gathered at the tasting room door. I felt a jolt of panic – something I had felt many times since we had given up relatively secure city jobs for farming in South-West France. I steeled myself, pulled the tasting-room door open, rushed in and closed it behind me before I got any wetter.

It felt safer inside the protective capsule of glass, stone, and wood. We had only harvested the Sauvignon Blanc, about a tenth of our harvest. The rest was still on the vines and not quite ready. My brain flipped through potential outcomes. The only acceptable one was for the hail to stop.

Hail was more frequent than it had been a decade before. Global warming was creating unstable weather, including more storms. I felt my stomach twist.

Sean was going through the motions of the tasting, trying to ignore the unfolding disaster. The darkest part of the storm was still the other side of Saussignac. In a matter of minutes, it would hit us. There was nothing we could do. Sean commented on this aroma and that tannin, what he had done in the vineyard and in the winery. It was like making small talk while watching a car crash.

The dark mass boiled out as if an invisible force holding it had let go. It rolled like angry water released from a dam wall over Saussignac Castle. The hail drumbeat on the roof increased. We stopped talking. The noise outside reached fever pitch; rain and hail pounding, wind thrashing trees and vines relentlessly.

I felt like our lives were suspended over a void. We were tightrope walkers high on a wire, nothing below us. In a few minutes our harvest could be shredded. Long seconds passed, then the mass split into two and the destructive darkness raced away; one part towards Gageac-et-Rouillac in the east, the other to Razac-de-Saussignac in the west. The battering of the hail calmed, then stopped.

'Holy smokes,' I said.

'That was close,' said Sean.

Christophe was wide-eyed.

'I wonder what the damage is?' I reflected.

'Not as bad as it could have been,' replied Sean as he rinsed the glasses.

'We should go and check now.'

'Relax,' said Sean. 'If we see it now or in ten minutes it's not going to make any difference.'

I swallowed my panic and tried to concentrate on the wine.

The sun came out. Like the returning light, the last wine was golden: our Saussignac botrytis dessert wine.

'This is very good,' said Christophe after taking a sniff and a sip. 'It's like a *trockenbeerenauslese*.'

Trockenbeerenauslese means 'dried berry selection' in German. It is their term for wine made from botrytis noble rot grapes. Making a diverse range of wines made us better teachers for the custom wine courses and Wine Spirit Education Trust (WSET) approved programmes we ran under the banner of French Wine Adventures, the wine school and wine tours side of the business. It was a diversification I felt particularly grateful for after the hail. Christophe took another sip, savoured it, spat into the spittoon, then set his glass down.

'Your wines are great. Real *terroir*. I would love to stay and talk more but I know you're anxious to check the grapes.'

He had a reserved Northern European way about him. We were in the midst of a crisis, and he acknowledged that but was calm.

'It is what it is,' said Sean philosophically. 'I think we missed the worst of it.'

We exchanged bottles with Christophe. The tradition of swapping wine with other winegrowers was one we cherished. Since becoming winemakers, we rarely drank wine made by someone we didn't know. It added a special dimension to our enjoyment of our favourite drink.

As we waved farewell, our minds were already in the vineyard. Before his car had turned up the hill to Saussignac I was pulling on my boots. Night was falling. We needed to get out there fast.

With a worker lamp in hand, we followed the track below our house, a long stone building covered in grey concrete. Beneath the seventies concrete that the locals called *crépi* we knew there were original cut stones that had been quarried on the farm. Removing it was one of many projects planned for the future.

The Dordogne Valley spread below us like a quilt of perfect country scenes. Vineyards, plum orchards, forests, and pasture were sewn together, patterns of green and gold with the river in the middle. The scene looked peaceful and safe. Yet the village of Mardenne's only water source was one of 500 community wells that had special project status because it was so polluted by local farmers' activities. A programme of phone calls and meetings had been initiated to cajole farmers to stop using the legal poisons that were showing up in the water. So far it wasn't working. A recent analysis of the town's water showed the herbicide level so high that there wasn't a scale for it. A farmer had weed-killed a field hours before a storm and it had washed the herbicide directly into the community's water. The herbicide was glyphosate, classified by the World Health Organization (WHO) as 'probably' carcinogenic. It was still legal in the EU and should have been banned long before. Mardenne's well showed glyphosate but also traces of chemicals that had been banned for more than ten years, including atrazine and arsenic. Atrazine was a popular herbicide in the twentieth century but has been shown to be a persistent endocrine disrupter and carcinogen. Arsenic is a famous poison – it was a favourite method for murder in the Middle Ages and the Renaissance – but was considered a great idea as an agricultural pesticide in the 1900s. It is a poison that can kill. In smaller doses, it leads to nervous-system disruption that can cause diseases like Alzheimer's. I was grateful our tap water didn't come from there.

Our local district of Saussignac was slowly transforming to organic farming. A large percentage of winegrowers had already converted: around 20 percent of the vineyard surface area, compared to an average in France of around 4 percent at the time. Local farmers had started on the road to organic for different personal reasons. One neighbouring couple were driven to find an alternative to chemical farming when their five-year-old daughter got leukaemia. Their research concluded that systemic chemicals were behind their daughter's terrible disease, and they went organic. With treatment their daughter recovered. Another close friend went organic after realising chemical farming was bad for the quality of his wine and for his long-term yield despite what the agricultural advisers said. Not surprisingly, many 'advisers' were connected to the sale of agricultural chemicals.

I set aside my thoughts about Mardenne's water calamity and focused on our immediate one – the hail. The vines were covered in green plumage. Without needing to get closer, I already knew the storm had not been as devastating as one in St-Émilion a couple of years before. Then the vines were hit so hard that it looked like winter, the leaves and just-set fruit shredded off the trellis, leaving only the solid wood and cane structures like emaciated skeletons.

But, given the fragile state of our almost ripe fruit, even a small amount of hail could wreck our crop. The old Semillon vines down the east-facing slope looked ruffled. I stepped into a row and lifted leaves to scrutinise the grapes.

'No broken skin here,' I said, feeling a flood of relief.

'Nor here,' said Sean, doing the same on the next row. 'A bit windblown, that's all.'

'Thank God.' I popped a grape into my mouth. After chewing and tasting the skin and pulp, I spat the pips into my hand to look at the colour. There was a line of bright green down the centre. They were almost ready. In a few days the green would diminish, and the pips would brown and start to taste a little nutty instead of bitter astringent.

'We should pick on Thursday as planned,' said Sean after doing the same.

Each year we started harvest with a vague idea of which days would be ideal for each grape and then adjusted our plan based on the weather and development of the grapes. We were on target.

We kept walking, hurrying but stopping every few rows to check the bunches. The vines changed from Semillon to Sauvignon Blanc.

'The further we go the more roughed up the vines look,' I said. 'Thank God this Sauvignon is safe in the winery.'

Sean nodded.

'There are perforated leaves here,' he said, lifting one to show me.

My anxiety rose. Around the corner was Hillside Merlot, one of our most valuable vineyards, old vines that created our highest quality reds. I found grapes with broken skin in the first row.

'We've been hit,' I said, my heartbeat pounding in my ears. My mind raced to the implications.

Sean looked up from the next row.

'Here too. It looks bad but I don't think it's as serious as you might think. Also, we hand-pick this parcel so we can remove any damaged grapes when we harvest.'

'But won't damage bring bugs? And rot?' I asked.

'It could. But is there enough to hit the emergency button? This is one of our best red vineyards. We need it for red. If we pick now, it will only be good for rosé. Let's count how many damaged grapes we find on the last two rows where it's worst.'

We each took a row.

'Around one broken grape every three bunches,' I said as I reached the end of mine.

'You see. Less than one percent,' said Sean. 'It was the same for me. Definitely not enough to warrant picking when it isn't ripe.'

'But even a little damage could bring rot.'

'That's a risk,' said Sean. 'Let's go and check the other Merlot.'

Feeling a little light-headed with a combination of anxiety and relief, we crossed the semicircle of grass cupped by a curved wall of limestone that we called the amphitheatre, home to a giant fig tree. It presided over the area like a dark-green wise woman. Its gorgeous, lush leaves offered deep shade; its fresh fruit fed us for weeks in season and its jam the rest of the year. Through the summer its tantalising scent reached way over to the vineyard, an aroma so uplifting that French perfume producers sold a home fragrance called *Sous le Figuier* - Under the Fig Tree. Passing it, I couldn't resist picking a fig despite our haste. I was a figaholic. When Sean visited the farm for the first time and told me it had copious fig trees, I declared, 'It was made for us!' If it had figs, I was ready to buy.

A few metres past the fig, a staircase of wood and stone wound up the cliff from the amphitheatre to the tasting room. Clambering up the uneven steps I thought of Ad and his son Adrian, friends from Holland, who had made the steps. Back then there was no tasting room, wine school or Wine Lodge accommodation. Now the view above us was filled by two structures built on to the original stone walls of an abandoned workshop, pigsty, and stables from the nineteenth century. Each time I saw the buildings I felt a wave of gratitude. Their oak frames were works of art, like the ever-changing views they offered on to the vineyards. We reached the top and stopped.

'What a view,' said Sean. 'Even after the storm.'

We took in the scene for a few moments, then he sighed deeply and said, 'We had better get on or the light will be gone.'

That sigh was the first sign of how worried he was. It said so much about the care, attention and sweat that had gone into the vineyard and the disillusion that the grapes could be destroyed in a few minutes. Even if the damage was slight, the hail was a reminder of how fragile we were in the face of nature.

To keep up with Sean's long stride, my fast walk broke into a trot. We passed our herb *potager* kitchen garden, and turned towards Saussignac following the grassy track that ran alongside baby Cabernet Sauvignon vines we had planted three years before. Setting up the half hectare vineyard had taken tenacity – first to get the vineyard-planting rights, part of an archaic quota system, then to establish the vines. Like the buildings, it was a vote for the future.

We reached the end of the baby vines and the start of the last Merlot vineyards.

'The same procedure as the last vineyard?' I asked, using a phrase from a favourite film, *Dinner for One*.

'The same procedure,' said Sean, giving me a weak smile – another sign that he was worried.

'What do you think?' I asked as we reached the end.

'I think the arguments are the same though it's clearly worse. We'll lose more by jumping the gun and turning it into rosé than by waiting and removing the damaged grapes when we hand-pick. I'll do some research on what we can do to limit rot. A clay spray can help the healing but this close to harvest I'm not sure there's much we can do.'

A little further on, we reached our last triangle of Merlot. It was worse again.

'What will we do?' I asked.

'This vineyard isn't big enough to call the machine out and picking by hand with just the two of us isn't viable. Anyway, it would be such a small volume it would cost more to harvest than it would generate. We may have to forget this section,' said Sean. 'We'll see closer to harvest.'

I nodded. It was a tiny area, but we were a small producer and every grape mattered.

Beyond the triangle were another five rows of Sauvignon Blanc picked that morning. It was the most southerly point of our farm and it looked battered. I held my hands together in a gesture of gratitude to the sky, thankful we had harvested it before the storm struck.

As we walked back, we went through our options again. Sean was adamant that we shouldn't do anything and that there wasn't enough damage to jump the gun. I reticently agreed.

That night after dinner and saying goodnight to our daughters, I turned back my old sleeping bag that served as our duvet and heard the sound of harvest machines clattering and beeping high-pitched warning signals in the surrounding vineyards. Sean opened our bedroom window to close the shutters. The smell of the night, filled with harvest aromas of fresh grapes and crushed leaves, rushed into the room. I loved those aromas, but they brought a flutter of nerves. As winegrowers the month of September always held a hint of promise and nervous anticipation.

Our neighbour's courtyard lit up. His tractor and trailer rattled back from the vineyard. A chill ran down my spine. He was emergency-harvesting everything on a Saturday night because of the hail.

'Maybe we have underestimated the damage,' I said. 'Perhaps we should be harvesting.'

'I don't think so,' said Sean. 'We checked the grapes. We know the state of them. Anyway, like I said, we'll hand-pick those sections and remove the damaged grapes at harvest. Our neighbours machine-harvest so they don't have that option.'

He was probably right but the noise of the harvest machines made me doubt. Maybe they knew something we didn't.

'You saw how that cloud split,' added Sean. 'We were lucky. The vineyards the other side of Saussignac were hit worse than us.'

We stood in the dark, observing, our arms just touching. The bright lights of a harvester lit up the vines nearest the village and the clattering started again. Sean took a deep breath, sighed, reached for the shutters, and closed them decisively as if to say, 'Don't say another word.'

That night I thrashed back and forth, unable to sleep with the noise of the machines. I flushed hot and cold and wondered if I was getting sick. As soon as it was light enough, I went out to check again. The damage was there, but no worse than the night before. Our equilibrium was finely balanced. I was passionate about wine and organic farming but the uncertainty of life as a farmer could grind you down. Sometimes I felt like yelling 'stop'. But stopping the train we were on, especially in the middle of harvest, was not possible. There was no emergency brake.

CHAPTER 2

Harvest Thrills

The cold pre-dawn air stung my nostrils and the gravel crunched under my boots as I crossed the courtyard. Above me the sky was brilliant with stars. I could see Sean's outline through the insulation curtain of the winery. Sensing my arrival, he looked through a slit and inclined his head to listen.

'He's on his way,' he said, his ears picking up the harvest machine's whine across the valley.

I felt a flutter of adrenalin.

Sean dropped the curtain. I stepped forward and put my head through to see him blast a final jet of rinsing water over the vat destined for the day's Semillon. Then he attached the harvest pipe that would move fresh harvest from trailer to vat with elastic guy ropes.

A roar in the courtyard announced the arrival of the three-metre-tall harvester. It lit up the darkness like a cruise ship. Benoît, the driver, waved and climbed down the ladder to ground level. We exchanged the obligatory kisses and a few words about the harvest. After explaining where we were harvesting, I ran ahead to indicate the rows, marked with baby-pink Lycra bows, a tradition at Château Feely. He gave me a big smile then dissolved into giggles before straightening up and earnestly calibrating the machine.

He was setting the height and width of the rows but also more sophisticated information like the grape variety. Given the varietal, the machine would know the weight range of the grapes. For example, a typical Cabernet Sauvignon grape is smaller and weighs less than a Merlot grape. The sorting system inside would vacuum away the bits that weighed less than the lower point of the set range, while the sticks, whole bunches and other parts that were larger and weighed more would be caught by the sorting grille and vibrated to the back to be sorted into whole clusters to be de-stemmed and waste to be ejected. It was sophisticated equipment worth the equivalent of a modest house in France.

I jogged back up to the winery and found Sean climbing down from the scaffolding we had set up beside the vat.

'Everything's ready,' he said. 'Let's watch the progress so we know when to get into position.'

From the terrace we watched the machine lumbering down the vineyard like a high-tech dinosaur. It straddled the row and shook the vines with metal bow-shaped arms that ran parallel across the inside, making the grapes fall into a conveyor belt of silicon baskets and leaving the stems behind. A stream of rejected matter exited the sorting system at the back, creating a green, brown, yellow and gold cascade that shimmered in the rear lights.

We knew that the stream contained critter collateral - lizards, mice, snakes, and insects - and some were making it into the harvest bins despite the sorting – another reason we wanted to move to hand-harvesting everything. We didn't enjoy machine-harvesting but economically and organisationally it was the only option for our whites, rosé, and everyday red at the time. We were committed to a ten-year cycle with the harvest machine cooperative, so we were stuck. Already by hand-picking the top reds and the dessert wine we weren't using what we paid for each year. No 'get out' or flexibility was a downside to joining a machine cooperative, something we only realised once we were in.

I took a deep breath. At harvest time we were stretched even more than usual. We expected to finish in time for me to take our daughters, Sophia and Ellie, to school and to allow time to change into more suitable attire for welcoming guests for a day of wine school. Sean was focused on the culmination of his year's work in the vineyard while I kept up the wine tours and classes and shoehorned harvest in alongside the stream of administration and emails generated by our growing business.

We stood quietly for a moment. At the top of the next row the harvester turned back on to the main track.

'Let's go,' said Sean. 'We don't want to keep him waiting.'

The harvester pulled into position and Sean backed the tractor up behind him. From the pavement of our house, I was perfectly positioned to see how well aligned the tractor and harvester were but also well away so I wouldn't be crushed. Safety was always in our minds.

Every year farmers died in the process, either by a false step with a machine, falling from the top of a vat or ladder, electrocution, or asphyxiation from the carbon dioxide given off in fermentation.

Sean and Benoît lined up and prepared to empty the bins. It was almost right but I could see that some grapes would hit the lip of the trailer and be lost. I yelled and held my hand up. Benoît inclined the left bin then saw me and stopped the tip just in time. Sean pulled away and reversed back in. It was perfect. I gave a thumbs up, and the harvest flowed smoothly across. The harvester took off again, as I returned to the winery to watch Sean back the trailer into the entrance. The next step was connecting the trailer to the harvest pipe that would transfer the grapes to the vat. It was always a tough connection.

'Feck!' said Sean. 'Doesn't this make you dream of hand-harvesting?'

'Too right,' I said, panting with the effort of holding a pipe that was the thickness of a rugby player's thigh, with heavy metal ends, while Sean tried to close the join.

'Are you sure we have the right connector for this trailer?'

Sean gave me a withering look and cussed again.

The pipe got the message and clamped on.

He reached into the tractor cabin and switched on the power take-off (PTO) shaft that turned the auger - the screw conveyor - of the trailer. It hummed to life and fresh harvest began pumping into the pipe. The first splat hit the vat next to me and was followed by a rhythmical flow. Satisfied that the load was transferring smoothly, I climbed down the scaffolding. As I stepped on to the ground, the sound of pouring stopped. The auger was still going but harvest was not flowing through. I waved to Sean and climbed back up the scaffolding.

'Nothing's coming through,' I shouted and held my fingers in a cross.

A couple of years before, the auger was jammed by a metal hook, and we had had to empty a trailer-load by hand. We learned the lesson well and hadn't used those metal hooks to repair the trellising since.

Sean turned off the trailer.

'It can't be a hook – it's still turning,' he said as if reading my mind. 'Stay up there. I'll turn it back on and up the power – maybe it needs a little more encouragement.'

Power made no difference. The auger just macerated our precious harvest more furiously for no result.

I shook my head, feeling a tiny stream of panic. Benoît would soon be back with the second load.

Sean stopped the tractor and came around to join me.

'It must be the angle of the pipe. The slope's too steep,' he said. 'We have to lift it.'

Sean crossed the winery floor to fetch an A-frame ladder then set it up at the middle point, raising the centre of the pipe half a metre above the original position on a stack of wooden pallets.

'Maybe that'll do it.'

'Could it really be as simple as that?' I said.

'Basic physics,' said Sean. 'You climb up there and make sure it stays in position.'

'Easy for you to say,' I said, clambering back up the scaffolding to hang on to the pipe. With hundreds of kilograms of harvest pumping through, it could be as dangerous as a python.

Sean looked back to check I was in place and started the auger. Harvest throbbed through the pipe, the ladder stayed firmly in position and, seconds later, grapes splattered into the vat. I gave a thumbs up and a relieved smile. In minutes the load was finished. I felt like we had climbed a mountain. Sean turned off the PTO.

I relished that there was no noise for a moment then realised the vineyard below the winery, where the harvester should have been working, was silent. I flung open the winery shutters. The dawn had painted a strip of apricot and yellow across the top of Gageac hill. Above it a range of blues progressed up through the sky still filled with stars. But below the beauty the machine was stopped about ten metres into a vineyard row.

'Feck,' said Sean, looking over my shoulder. 'We'd better go and see what's happening.'

Breaking harvest part way was bad for us work-wise, and it meant oxidation for the juice that was already in the harvest-machine bins. Out in the vineyard, the harvested grapes were not protected by inert gas as they were in the winery.

'Maybe we should take some sulphur dioxide,' I said.

'I'll come back if it's necessary,' replied Sean. 'The earlier we start dosing, the more it needs.'

Sulphur dioxide, marked as 'sulphites' on wine bottles, is a preservative for wine but it is also like a drug – if we started now our juice would be addicted, and we preferred to use as few sulphites as possible.

Sean closed the insulation curtain and the metal sliding door of the winery, and we jogged round to where the harvester was.

Benoît was pulling at a trellis pole that poked out of the machine at a nasty angle. The section of vines above him and all its trellising had been ripped out.

'A part of the trellis got caught,' said Benoît. 'I stopped as soon as I realised but it was already too late for them.'

He pointed to the uprooted vines, ancients that had lived happily on this hillside for nearly seventy years. I could almost hear them crying.

Sean moved to help Benoît pull the pole. They yanked it with all their shared force, and nothing moved.

'It's too far in. We can't pull it out,' said Sean.

Something about the situation made me laugh. The craziness of it, the sadness of the dying vines, the phrase Sean had just used. Sean glared at me.

'Do you have a chainsaw?' asked Benoît.

'*Bien sûr*,' replied Sean and turned to go and fetch it.

'I am very sorry,' said Benoît.

'Don't worry, Benoît, it's only a few vines,' I said, trying to downplay the situation since I could see he felt bad. 'I hope the machine isn't damaged.'

He pulled a face that said it all. It was the start of harvest season. The CUMA, our agricultural cooperative, needed both machines working. From us he was due to go to another farm and then another. It wouldn't only be our morning that was affected. The machines worked around 16 hours a day – two driver shifts and sometimes more.

In minutes Sean was back, large chainsaw in hand. He and Benoît discussed the best approach then the tell-tale buzz split the dawn and the pole succumbed piece by piece. They worked like surgeons, careful not to damage themselves or the harvester. The chainsaw went silent.

'At first glance the harvester looks OK,' said Benoît.

Sean rolled away the wires and the uprooted vines, and Benoît leaped up the ladder into the cabin. He drove ten metres then stopped, leaned out and gave us a thumbs up.

'Crisis over,' said Sean. 'Back to work.'

'We've been out here half an hour at least. Won't our fruit be oxidised from sitting exposed to the air for this extra time?' I said.

'There was very little in the bins. He had only done a couple of rows when it happened and it's still cool. It'll be all right,' said Sean.

In the winery I kept looking out of the window to check on Benoît's progress. With the delay we would finish close to when the tour group was due to arrive.

The sun was up when he came back. The transfer went smoothly and while Sean backed the trailer up to the winery and set about preparing for the next part, I signed Benoît's papers.

'You can apply to the CUMA for insurance for the damage,' said Benoît. 'It must have been a loose trellis pole.'

'Well, thank goodness the machine is working fine,' I said, ignoring the delicate pass of the blame.

We checked the vineyard for loose vines and poles before the harvest machine passed. It was possible that one had seemed OK to us but wasn't up to a thwack by a three-ton harvest machine.

'Would you like an espresso before you go?' I asked.

With the pressure I felt about the day ahead, I already regretted making the offer. As if sensing my stress, Benoît unusually declined.

'I need to get on and I know you do too,' he said, nodding his head in the direction of Sean waiting for me. Our harvest couldn't be delayed another second.

'Thank you so much, Benoît,' I said and kissed him on each cheek.

He waved farewell from the top of the ladder then swung into the cabin and closed the door. The harvester whined and beeped, its tyres turning up the gravel of the courtyard, then took off up the road, its bulk dwarfing the adult cherry trees at the entrance to the farm.

'Come on, come on,' shouted Sean.

Back in the winery, I climbed the scaffolding to hold the pipe that was now finely balanced over the A-frame ladder and Sean started the auger. In minutes, most of the harvest had made it into the vat and Sean was scraping the fruit from the edges of the harvest trailer. He chased them with a bucket of water, the extra pressure from behind necessary to get some of the last fruit through. Then he switched off the auger and tractor. Jointly we unhitched the pipe and hiked it, still heavy with fruit, into a food grade bin to collect the last few litres.

I rolled the nitrogen gas bottle – almost the same size as me – to the tank as Sean climbed up, then passed him the gas wand. Nitrogen is an inert gas and created a blanket to protect our harvest from oxidation. He filled the tank with gas then handed it back to me and I rolled the bottle back into position.

Seven years of harvest and our motions were like a choreographed ballet. We moved automatically through the activities; no need to speak. Each year we improved our set-up and became more familiar with what we needed to do. We were old hands.

But the word 'hand' reminded me how important it was to not let familiarity allow our guard to drop. Sean had lost a third of his finger to the auger of the trailer we were using that day. It was the last day of our first harvest. Sean's finger still ached at times; the part that was missing itched like it was still there. It had recently started to grow a sharp bit of bone out of the side of the stub. He rubbed it subconsciously.

'We should have a cup of tea,' I said. 'I need to check on the girls anyway.'

Since the accident we had learned to take appropriate breaks during intense days. Being overtired created lapses in concentration that could be fatal in a winery.

In the kitchen, Sophia and Ellie were putting on their shoes, preparing to go to school. They had dressed and eaten breakfast. Since they were too small to remember, they had had to get on with their lives like tiny adults when we were in the midst of moments like harvest. I gave them each a hug and turned on the kettle.

'Are your bags ready?' I asked.

They nodded sagely.

The kettle boiled as Sonia, our neighbour, arrived. I quickly poured water into the two cups – black tea for me and rooibos for Sean – then went out to kiss Sophia and Ellie goodbye and help them up into Sonia's car. She had saved us on many occasions, doing the school run for me at short notice.

'*Bonne journée!*' I shouted as they drove off.

In the kitchen plumes of steam rose over the cups and the fragrance of the two teas mingled in the air. I poured a drop of milk into mine and took the cups outside.

Sean and I sat on a pallet and sipped our tea.

'I'll be OK doing the clean-up on my own,' he said. 'You get ready for your group. I can't help with the prep today.'

'I'll be busier than a one-legged man in a butt-kicking competition,' I said and laughed as I pictured the saying, a favourite of one of my sister's exes.

In the garden, the last of the baby tomatoes hung on the vines. I picked a few red orbs for my basket then tasted one and marvelled at the flavour. The view of the Dordogne Valley from the *potager* was like a scene from a fantasy film; mist swirled across the surface, parallel eddies snaking away from the river in constant movement. Immediately below us in the flat of the valley, two blue firs and the château of our neighbour's property peeked up through the mist as if they were floating on an enchanted cloud. I took in the view like a quenching drink of peace, then popped another tomato into my mouth, picked a few more for my basket and went inside to change into a dress and pearls. I slicked on lipstick and checked my face for sunscreen marks.

In the tasting-room kitchen, I set eight plates on the preparation table then cut the cheeses for the lunch and made the salad dressing. As I placed the cheeses back in the fridge, a minibus pulled up outside. My group had arrived, right on time.

For the next few hours, I was engrossed in sharing my passion for wine, *terroir*, vineyard, organic and biodynamic agriculture. After serving lunch, I jogged across the courtyard and wolfed down a slice of bread and tomato. Sean was stretched out on the sofa in the lounge for a half-hour siesta. Doing physical work all day, he needed a moment to recharge. I raced back to continue the lunch service and afternoon session.

The group left with warm farewells, promising to return and to share our address with friends. They were happy. The feedback forms on the table filled me with a warm sensation. Many said they left with a new appreciation for wine and particularly for organic wine. Of everything we were doing, this gave me the most satisfaction. It didn't feel like work. I loved it.

The cleaning up was another matter. I stacked as many glasses and plates as would fit into the dishwasher and set it to go so that I could unload it and reload before closing up for the night.

It was time to fetch Sophia and Ellie. I grabbed our dog Dora's lead and she barked with excitement.

We trotted up the last row of the hail-damaged Merlot to the village so I could see what it was like five days after the event. I didn't see any flies hovering or pick up smells of vinegar or rot as we passed, but there was no time to look closely – we were late. Dora sensed the urgency and raced ahead, pulling me up the hill like a sled dog.

Sophia and Ellie were waiting at the school gate, the last to be collected. They gave me a look of reproach.

'*Mes excuses pour le retard*,' I apologised to Krystel, who ran the after-school service.

'*Pas de problème*,' she replied, her tone implying a little extra flexibility was allowed for winegrowers in the thick of harvest.

I kissed the girls on their foreheads.

'Sorry I'm late,' I said. 'Today has been hectic.'

'Don't worry, Mum,' said Sophia.

Ellie gave me a glare that said, 'Don't do it again.'

'So, how's life?' I asked as we set off back down the hill.

'OK,' replied Sophia.

'*Bof*,' responded Ellie.

Despite their downbeat replies I felt happy, filled with gratitude for where we were; for the soft autumn air; for the joy of walking; the grand panorama of the valley spread below us.

'Let's sing!' I said and waited a moment then started a song. 'There is fun everywhere, Olé olé olé, Swing your arms in the air, Olé olé olé.'

Ellie joined me and we sang the refrain again, then she added a section, '*et fait caca par terre*' which translated as 'and do a poo on the ground'. In French it worked perfectly with the rhyme of the song. I felt a little disgusted but found myself laughing.

'One of my friends made it up,' said Ellie gleefully. Her class was of an age where potty humour was a hit.

'Oh no,' I said, laughing all the more. 'I'll never be able to sing it normally again.'

We turned down the second Merlot row and I stopped to check bunches and taste grapes every few metres. A few had fuzzy rot and I felt a pinch of anxiety. We were still a couple of weeks off the ideal moment for harvesting the reds. It would take some nerve to hold out.

As we entered the courtyard that formed the U-shaped centre of the house and outbuildings, Sean came out of the winery, arms wide, and the girls ran to give him hugs and kisses.

'Make yourselves a *goûter*,' I said. 'A drink, some fruit, some bread and jam, then do your homework. OK?'

'Yes, Mum,' said Sophia.

'Help Ellie if she needs it,' I added.

We expected Sophia to take the lead since she was tiny. Now, at nine years old, she was super responsible. I knew

I could rely on her to do her homework without being asked, to get up on time, to have her breakfast and be ready. With Ellie, who was two years younger, it wasn't so certain. She found it hard to get up and needed follow-up supervision unless it was something she loved. She was timid with people she didn't know and rebellious at the same time, but she had an iron will and had been capable of staring down an adult at a couple of months old.

Leaving them to fend for themselves, I returned to my clean-up. After emptying and refilling the dishwasher and vacuuming the floor, it was 6.30 p.m. I had been on my feet almost non-stop for 14 hours. My dad was probably right with his 'if you keep going at this rate, you'll be dead before you retire' comment, no matter how much I loved it.

Sean had a long day too. After I left, he pressed the Semillon and started cold settling the juice. Cleaning the press and all the equipment meant he would finish even later than me. We needed to find a solution to being overstretched but the cost of hiring someone, even at the minimum wage, made it difficult despite the growing demand for our visits and our wines. I set the dishwasher to run again, all the while thinking about what to do. To make the business financially sustainable we needed to sell out and sell everything in the bottle at higher prices than we were at that moment. Selling more wine would take time I didn't have. We needed another pair of hands; to get that we needed more income. It was a chicken-and-egg situation I knew I wouldn't solve immediately, particularly since Sean and I took turns to cook, and it was my night. I locked up the tasting room.

Realising the time, I turned to run to the house, tripped on the outside mat and flew across the gravel. I came down hard, knocking the breath out of myself. Head pounding, I picked my body up. I was dazed, and my knees and hands were bleeding, but there didn't appear to be any serious damage. Inside the house, I cleaned myself off, and found my lip was bleeding too. I disinfected the scrapes.

Oblivious to the flying mum act that had taken place, the girls had finished their homework and were preparing to play a game of Wii on our ancient, fat TV. I left them to it and went to prepare dinner. I didn't know what to cook but almost everything started with onions chopped and sweated in butter, so I did that. Then I saw a bag of Sean's home-made tomato sauce in the fridge. I threw that in with crushed garlic, a pinch of sugar and salt, a twist of black pepper and a few sprigs of oregano from the garden and left the pan to simmer.

A pasta sauce like this needed a glass of Italian wine – for the sauce and for the chef. Taking a medieval-looking key from the cupboard, I strolled down to the wine cellar under the house. The ancient room filled me with awe at the weight of history, its solidity, and the bottles of wine – including our own from back vintages that were sold out. It was a crossroads of architectural history and wine. The back wall of perfectly cut square stones blackened with age dated, according to a local expert, to around 700, the time when a monastery was constructed in Saussignac. The other walls were 'young', dating to the fourteenth and eighteenth centuries respectively. I still found it hard to believe that it was ours and we were slowly building our own vineyard history in wine.

Our bottled history was modest compared to some of the *châteaux* I visited in St-Émilion - at Château Guadet they had vintages going back to 1914. We knew each one, down to details like 'Maeve and Conor were here for that harvest' or 'that was the year of the frost'. Each bottle was a tapestry of memories, of hiccups, and of successes. For all the angst of winegrowing, there was something profound about this *métier* - profession - where we worked with nature and made a living product that could last a lifetime.

The swap stock I had exchanged at the last organic wine fair for professionals was piled against the back wall. Like other fairs, it had been a good opportunity to meet other growers. In the dim light I rifled through bottles stacked in cardboard boxes.

'Perfect!' I said out loud, spotting a Chianti, the ideal match for my pasta supper. I lifted the bottle that recalled a frantic swap with a handsome Italian at the end of the show but not much else. I wouldn't tell Sean that. 'Horse piss,' he would say, 'and he probably wore pointy shoes.' Sean had a thing about pointy shoes. For him, they were a sign of a salesman, a slippery, shifty character, and an instant write-off for the unsuspecting wearer.

The wine was a young Chianti DOCG (*Denominazione di Origine Controllata e Garantita*), made with organic grapes, mostly Sangiovese with a little Merlot. Since 1996, under pressure from the success of renegade wines known as 'Super Tuscans', Chianti had allowed up to 20 percent of the blend to be international varieties like Cabernet Sauvignon, Merlot, and Syrah, also known as Shiraz in the new world.

'What's going on?' asked Sean, passing the open cellar door as he walked up from putting his last load of pressed grapes on the compost.

'Wine for tonight,' I said, holding up my treasure, without a word about the maker. I locked the cellar door.

'What happened to you?' Sean asked, noticing my lip then seeing my hands and knees.

I explained.

'You've got to slow down, Caro,' he said.

'Easy to say, not easy to do.'

'I know,' he replied.

We walked back up to the kitchen together.

The sauce bubbling on the stove filled the kitchen with delicious aromas of tomato and garlic. I took two glasses from the cupboard, pulled the cork, and poured, savouring the sound of the wine passing from bottle to glass.

My nose picked up a waft of cherry then I gave the glass a good swirl and sniffed again, this time more deeply, allowing the aromas to expand through my nasal passages and into my brain. Images of cherry, cinnamon, scrub herbs and tea formed. I took a sip and swished it around my mouth. On the palate it was light and fruity with good acidity.

'It's good,' said Sean.

'Not bad for a man with pointy shoes,' I responded.

Sean's face dropped, and I burst out laughing.

'He-he. Only joking.'

I crossed the courtyard for fresh parsley, snipped it into my sauce and served it on tagliatelle.

'Cheers, everybody!' I said, lifting my glass as I sat down. 'To a successful harvest!'

'Cheers, Mummy,' said Ellie, clinking her glass of elderflower juice and making eye contact then moving to do the same with Sophia and Sean.

We made our way around, careful not to cross each other in the process. It was a family ritual.

Eating together was a sacred moment but it was a weeknight, so we didn't linger. Sean had started a routine where Sophia and Ellie cleaned up. At the end of the meal, we got up and left them to it. It was precious extra time. I went to catch up on the emails that had come in through the day and Sean went to finish cleaning the winery. In amongst the work mail was one from a biodynamic truffle farm in Quercy, near Cahors, offering a truffling weekend in February. We farmed in the biodynamic way, like 'organic plus', so my ears pricked up.

To go biodynamic a farm must already be certified organic. In most farming – including vines – being organic means no chemical fertilisers, herbicides, systemic pesticides, or systemic fungicides. Put simply, biodynamics includes three additional elements. The first is to think of the farm as a whole farm system, a living ecosystem that can be self-sufficient. The second is working with the farmer's almanac, a calendar of the earth's movements in relation to the moon, planets, and constellations. Each cosmic entity is associated with one of the four elements: earth, water, air, and fire. By plotting them and their position in relation to our planet, the calendar identifies which element is strongest at a given moment. Each element is linked to a part of the plant: earth to root, water to leaf, air to flower, and fire to fruit. The ideal moment to do different activities is when its associated element is strongest. For example, we plant carrots on a root day, lettuce on a leaf day, roses on a flower day, tomatoes on a fruit day. We prefer to harvest our grapes on a fruit day. It sounds crazy but think of the effect of the moon on the tides of the sea. If it can move that volume of water, it's a seriously powerful force. Third, in biodynamics we use plant- and animal-based preparations and sprays, ideally from our farm, to aid the plants to grow and protect themselves.

I was a sceptic until I saw what a difference biodynamics made to our vineyard and to our wines. Since going biodynamic, we had decreased our dose of copper for combating downy mildew, one of the most dangerous fungal diseases in our region, from 6 kilograms per hectare, the maximum that was allowed at the time, to under 1.5 kilograms per hectare. With biodynamics, our vines were becoming more resistant to disease and our wines tasted better. Our experience made me want to visit more biodynamic farms.

St Amour's truffle weekend fell on our fifteenth wedding anniversary. In Dublin Sean and I went out every year to celebrate but since moving to France we hadn't been out to celebrate. This looked like an ideal opportunity to find out what the truffle hype was about, to learn from another biodynamic farm, and to catch up on years of missed celebrations. I knew our relationship needed attention. It was like anything – ignored for long enough, it would wither and die. Before I had time to talk myself out of it, I sent an email to book it.

Over the next month harvest progressed peacefully. We hand-picked the hailed Merlot on our annual vine shareholder weekend. Our diligent pickers carefully removed all rot. We lost a quarter in the sorting, but the result tasted good. With the worry about hail damage assuaged and visits calming with the cold season, I should have felt more relaxed but instead I felt on edge. I struggled to sleep and when I did, I had nightmares about dying. I flushed hot and cold and felt out of sorts. My temper flared at nothing. Sean remained calm. He swept the chimney of our wood-burning stove. Winter closed in. Soups and stews took over from salads and barbecues. Sophia and Ellie began working on their Christmas lists.

CHAPTER 3

Hunting Black Gold

Real Christmas came and went. It was one I chose to forget as Sean gifted me a household steam-cleaning machine. He must have missed the 'How to Avoid Divorce 101' course.

I considered cancelling the truffle weekend but decided that I deserved it even if he didn't. He was halfway through the winter pruning when I gave him the card for our truffle experience at St Amour for our anniversary.

'I hope you booked the truffle menu,' he said. 'No point in going truffle-hunting if we aren't going to eat truffles.'

I laughed nervously. He knew me too well and he didn't know how much the truffle menu cost. I had pre-booked the cheapest menu for both of us. I wanted to experience the place, but the cost made me hyperventilate.

On the appointed day, we delivered Sophia and Ellie, bubbling with excitement about a night of fun with their friends Florence and Martha of *Famille* Moore. Dave and Amanda had transformed their run-down farmhouse, bought a couple of years before, into a *manoir*. There was no trace of the fire that had ravaged their living room when they looked after our daughters during our trip to California a couple of years before. The stink that persisted for months was gone and the chimney that caused the fire had been erased. The progress they had made on the house and on the wine their vineyard produced was extraordinary.

After goodbye kisses, our daughters scampered off to play with their friends without giving us a second glance. As we drove away, I felt sad to leave them. It was strange to be going away for a lovers' weekend.

St Amour was expecting us mid-afternoon, so we had time for sightseeing. En route via district roads the landscape slowly changed from vines to grains and pasture. We passed Monflanquin, a *bastide* fortified town, bound by stone ramparts and an awe-inspiring medieval city gate.

The further inland we travelled, the colder it became. The houses were more enclosed; windows were smaller; roofs steeper, and colours more sombre. At Fumel, we parked the car and walked up through the village, around the famous castle, and its terraced gardens with panoramic views of the Lot River. We looked for a guided visit, but it was deserted and silent, typical for winter in rural South-West France. A few boards told the history of the nobility of the castle, but it was bone dry and I struggled to concentrate.

Feeling hungry we wandered back down, looking for a place to eat. I wanted something light and Sean wanted something solid after pruning for two hours that morning.

We found a dark tavern that offered both and was the only place open.

Fumel was on the border of the region we were heading for: the Quercy, famous for Cahors wine, a strong and tannic red made from at least 70 percent Malbec with blending partners of Merlot and Tannat. The region's food did a good impersonation of the Dordogne and was famous for all things duck. We knew it was best to stick with regional specialities that were certain to be local products. Sean selected *confit de canard* - duck confit - and a glass of local wine, and I chose *salade de Quercy*. It looked exactly like a Périgourdine salad: a pile of fresh lettuce and tomato loaded with duck gizzards, smoked duck breast, walnuts and a vinaigrette dressing made with walnut oil. Both delivered more than we expected. We were fortified, happy, and ready to truffle.

In the tiny village of Lariolle a sign pointed us up a track to St Amour. It was remote and isolated, a cluster of houses rather than a village. We wound up to a parking area in front of imposing gates. A dark green Porsche, a black Mercedes sports car and a red Audi cabriolet were already parked up. We squeezed our Mazda into the last space.

'Perhaps we should have brought the Louis Vuitton,' I said, taking out my kitbag received as a corporate gift years before.

Sean laughed, rubbing his old leather shoes with a cloth. He made to close the car boot.

'Don't forget the bag with the boots. We need them to go truffling,' I said.

'No way am I taking that old shopping bag in here,' said Sean. 'I'll come back for them later.'

Wrapped in coats and scarves, our bags slung over our shoulders, we passed through the gate and followed a stone path up to the main building, a double-storey Quercy farmhouse. A wide set of stairs led to a terrace where the door opened into a dining-room reception area. We heard voices and a slight blonde woman, dressed in jeans and collared shirt, appeared from their direction.

'*Bonjour.* Caro et Sean Feely,' I said, introducing us both.

'*Bonjour et bienvenue. Inés,*' she said and shook our hands. '*Enchanté.*'

'Sorry we're a little late,' I said.

'*Pas de problème.* We're having tea. I'll show you to your room so you can install your bags then you must join us.'

We followed Inés down the steps and up another staircase to the terrace of a separate part of the farmhouse complex. She opened the door of a cosy-looking room and spread her arms in a gesture of welcome.

'Make yourselves at home. We don't have keys so just close the door behind you to keep the heat in. As soon as you are ready, please join us.'

The room was cold, but the bed had layers of inviting covers. Cream stone walls, a solid oak floor, and an exposed-beam ceiling, provided the backdrop for antique bedside tables, the large bed, a walnut armoire, a flame-coloured sofa, and a writing desk. I dropped my bag on to a chair and threw myself on the bed.

'Do you know truffles are aphrodisiacs?' I said, bouncing up and down to see how it felt.

'But you're on the entry-level menu that doesn't include truffles,' said Sean. 'Bad luck for you.'

We laughed. We had agreed that Sean would go for the middle menu that had some truffles, but I was going to stick to the lowest cost option.

I jumped up and looked into the bathroom.

'A bath! Total luxe!' At home one tiny shower room sufficed for four of us. When the Wine Cottage was empty in winter, I sometimes stole across to enjoy a bath, but since that part of the house wasn't heated, unless there were guests, it was pleasure tinged with pain.

'I'll get the boots,' said Sean.

The window looked onto vegetable gardens terraced down to a dam, fields, and forests. It was beautiful and organised. Sean returned, boots in hand, not a shopping bag in sight.

'Thanks,' I said, taking my old leather hiking boots from him. I pulled them on and did up the laces. 'We'd better get over there. I don't want to miss the truffling.'

'Hang on, let me finish reading this article about the place,' said Sean, sitting on the sofa with a file of press clippings in front of him.

'No, we need to go! You can read that later,' I said, grabbing his coat and pulling him like an excited kid.

'OK, OK! Don't forget to tell them I want the middle menu that includes truffles.'

Despite having lived in France for many years, Sean felt self-conscious talking French to people he didn't know. With friends he was at ease in the knowledge that they would accept his grammatical and pronunciation errors. In his lonely job in the vineyard, he didn't get to practise as much as I did, and he had started with less French than I had.

In reception the sound of voices led us to the next room. It looked like a Louis Vuitton winter advert: blazing log fire, long dining table and people outfitted in luxurious leather, fur, and fine fabric, sipping from delicate cups.

Inés introduced us to the three couples, Parisians retired to a quieter life in La Rochelle. I caught half of their names but even those I wasn't sure about. When we arrived in France, I had had to replay a voicemail message eleven times to take down the name and number. Since then, I had improved but traditional French names said quickly were still difficult to compute and more difficult to store. It was even more complex when people introduced themselves with surname then first name, as they were obliged to do at school.

Guillaume, Inés's husband, and also the farmer and chef, came through the kitchen door as she finished the introductions. We shook hands.

'*Enchanté*,' he said. 'Can I interest you in a coffee or something stronger before you go truffling? These gentlemen are enjoying a local prune liqueur.'

'A coffee sounds magic,' I said.

'Liqueur please,' said Sean.

'A good choice,' said a portly fellow dressed like a tsar.

Guillaume reappeared with a silver tray holding a tiny china cup and a tot glass.

'Is it possible to have a touch of milk?' I asked.

'Of course,' Inés replied and returned with a minute jug of cream.

In France there was seldom a *nuage de lait*, a cloud of milk, for coffee or tea. I poured and a rich yellow web spread through the dark brew. The powerful aroma drew me in; the coffee was delicious.

Guillaume moved to check a pot hanging over the fire. He adjusted the metal structure holding it, and, seeing me approach, explained.

'I can hang multiple pots and adjust their height according to the heat required. We can also roast a whole carcass or portions of meat.' He pointed to a spit and a rugby-ball sized metal cage, like a barbecue grill but round. I felt like I had stepped back several hundred years.

'Speaking of cooking, have you decided which menu you wish to book for tonight?' he said. 'While you are out, I will start my preparations.'

'Thanks for reminding me,' I said. 'I had booked the short menu, but Sean would like the middle menu.'

'Unfortunately, we can't offer different menus to people at the same table. We are a small team. You both need to book for the same menu. The short menu doesn't include truffles, and it seems a pity not to have truffles when you are here for the truffle weekend.'

Like any good Libra I deliberated for a moment, weighing the scales this way and that way, despite it being obvious which choice I had to make. We only had our fifteenth anniversary once in our lives.

'We'll go for the middle menu,' I said and glanced at Sean.

He was following the banter, oblivious to the fact that I would be having an aphrodisiac dinner too. The group – including Sean – was settling in, the effects of prune liqueur and the warmth of the fire manifesting magnificently. It looked like it would be difficult to get them to move.

'*Alors*, are you going truffling or not?' asked Guillaume, sensing the same thing.

'*Bien sûr!*' said the portly man's wife. 'Let's go!'

Wrapped in coats, scarves, hats, and gloves, we descended the terrace steps. The temperature had dropped another degree or two.

'Please wait here while I get the dogs,' said Inés.

She went up to an outbuilding above the main house and opened the gate. A large black short-haired cross and a young blonde Labrador ran out in glee.

'It's cold but it's going to get colder. Snow is forecast,' said Inés, pulling her jacket in.

I felt a shiver as I recollected our three-day siege in Burgundy due to exceptional snow a couple of years before.

Inés led us out of the main gate and up a farm track into the forest. A few minutes later, sensitive to the puffing of some of us, she stopped.

'We'll take a break so I can tell you some history of the truffle,' she said. 'The Quercy, the name given to this region, comes from the Latin word "quercus" for oak tree. Before organised agriculture, what thrived on the high limestone and poor soil, were oak trees. The truffle loves to live on the roots of oak trees, so the region became famous for it. At the end of the nineteenth century, the *paysans* in France harvested around 3,000 tons of truffles. Today it is a great year if we harvest 30 tons across the country. One hundred times less. Why this massive drop?' She looked around. 'Any ideas?'

'Chemical agriculture?' I asked.

'Yes, that is a key reason,' responded Inés. 'Any other suggestions?'

She glanced around the group, then continued.

'What Madame said is correct – truffles are fungi, and they need a living soil. In "modern" agriculture we use chemical fertiliser, systemic pesticides, and weedkiller; these kill the life in the soil and hence the truffles.'

The rest of the party had questioning expressions. She explained.

'For the magic of the truffle to occur we need a living soil and that means farming organically at a minimum. Here we farm biodynamically as a way to take the life in our soil to a level beyond organic.'

I knew Inés could go a lot further with that thought but, like me when I hosted a group where the majority hadn't considered what organic farming was, she realised delving into biodynamics would be a step too far.

'Our mode of living has also changed,' said Inés. 'For truffles to develop, the forest needs to be cleared of undergrowth. The light needs to reach the soil. In the past, people collected fallen branches for kindling; browsers like deer and goats cleared the undergrowth and fertilised the soil at the same time. The light and the clearing of the undergrowth and animal presence are important for truffles to thrive. Does it make sense?'

We nodded.

Inés paused a moment then said, 'Perhaps that's enough talking. Are you ready to see the truffles? The dogs are.'

They were racing back and forth, eager to get going like Dora, our dog, when I did visits at the vineyard.

'*On y va!*' Inés used the French term that means 'let's go' but directly translates as 'one goes there'.

The end of the forest formed a cathedral-like window that opened on to neatly manicured smaller trees. We stepped through it into a different world. The plateau rolled like a great undulating blanket covered in green stubble and dotted with truffle trees in perfect rows.

'*Ça y est!* Here we are! We keep the trees pruned so that there is light on the ground. You see here?' Inés pointed to a stone circle at the base of the nearest tree. 'This is *le brûlé*, the burnt; this plant-free zone means there are probably truffles developing here. It's a telltale sign. We had better hurry. We have to follow the dogs to find the truffles.'

Inés sped off after the dogs. We followed, walking fast but not feeling the urgency that she did. The air was so cold it chapped my air passages as it passed through to my lungs. It smelt clean and clear. A great cloud of mist formed with each out-breath. The plateau was dotted with white circles of limestone under each tree. It felt remote and wild. Apart from the intermittent sounds made by our group there was deep silence, no cars, no planes, no machines.

'Show me Bacchus, where is the truffle?' said Inés, bending over the black dog who was digging about a metre from the base of a tree.

He looked up expectantly.

'Look for it. Come on, look for it!' She pointed into the hole with her trowel.

He continued more frantically then lifted his head again. Inés scraped away some dirt.

'There it is! Good dog! Bravo, Bacchus,' she said, and gave him a treat from her pocket then took the truffle out of the hole. She refilled the hole with earth, rose and passed the truffle to the nearest person.

'Smell that and pass it round,' she said. 'Our black gold.'

I took the nugget from Sean's outstretched hand. It was the size of a large walnut, with a bumpy, dusty, dark-brown surface. I saw why chocolate truffles were called such. It felt weighty and good in my hand. I lifted it to my nose. As I breathed in, I closed my eyes. The smell was floral and earthy. It was like being transported to a field rich with late summer aromas and at the same time to the warm comfort of a winter fireside filled with umami notes of the finest *cèpes* – porcini - a meaty forest mushroom. It was like a connection between heaven and earth, between summer and winter. In that breath I understood the excitement of truffles and why they cost so much. Years before I bought a tiny jar of oil with a truffle the size of a one-cent piece for Sean as a gift. It cost a fortune. He judiciously seasoned scrambled eggs and a roast chicken with it. We enjoyed it but we didn't understand why it created such genuflection in the world of gastronomy. Now I knew. I reluctantly handed it back to Inés.

The dogs charged off again and started sniffing at the base of a tree about 20 metres further on. It was the young dog's turn. Cosette dug feverishly and soon found treasure, but she hadn't learned to give it to her mistress yet. Inés prised her mouth open, scolding all the while, and took the truffle, explaining to Cosette that finding it was good, but eating it was bad, and gave her a treat from her pocket.

Bacchus had found another spot and was digging like a dog in a cartoon, his paws whirring with limestone and clay flying out behind him. Inés ran over to him. Meanwhile, the younger dog had found a different spot, and this time, with Inés's attention taken by Bacchus, Cosette ate what she found, gobbling truffles worth more than gold like they were dog biscuits. I called to Inés. She left one of the others to watch Bacchus and ran over to Cosette to salvage a piece of black gold from her jaws.

'We have to be vigilant and it's difficult with two dogs, but while she's learning I have to take them out together,' said Inés. 'It's best to be at least two with two dogs.'

Both dogs had taken off again, the older dog Bacchus streaking back up the slope towards the track that ran along the edge of the plateau. We raced after him and Inés called Cosette.

'It's extraordinary!' I said to Inés as I trotted next to her. 'From how far away can they smell the truffles?'

'Oh, we are not sure, but I think about thirty metres. Perhaps more,' she said.

As if to prove her point, Bacchus swerved into another row and came to a halt about thirty metres further on. He started digging and Inés caught up just in time to save the next nugget. It was like a strange game of hide-and-seek. She turned the metal bucket to show us how many she already had, a good five-centimetre layer of truffles of all sizes.

'How much are those truffles worth?' I asked.

'I don't know,' said Inés.

'It looks like about half a kilogram,' said the portly man. 'At least five hundred euro.'

'Phew!' I said. 'That's a good day's work for the dogs.'

'Yes, I think we have enough for today. The next section is young trees – there are no truffles there yet. We're experimenting with different companion plants between the truffle trees. We've made the rows wide enough to cultivate wheat between them. There are two benefits: the wheat aerates the soil with its root system, and we get to harvest wheat that is delicately perfumed with truffle. It's getting really cold, so we'll head back now,' said Inés as we reached a limestone track that dropped down off the plateau.

We followed her down a descent so steep it was almost vertical. I took teeny steps to keep my balance and hung on to Sean's hand. To our left and right the slopes were packed with trees holding the soil in place and stopping erosion. At the bottom a road took us back along the valley floor.

'We used to keep pigs, the traditional black pig of Gascony,' said Inés, pointing to an abandoned pigsty in the trees. 'They lived free and wild in this forest. But it became too much work with everything else that we were doing and made it difficult to travel so we decided to focus on truffles and hospitality. Now we have partners that raise the pigs as we would, and we do the maturation of the hams and some other pork products. You will taste them later. We grow grain and sunflowers over there.' She pointed to a flat fertile field. 'We use local products in our cuisine, many of them directly from our farm.'

We continued chatting as we walked back. I was keen to understand as much as I could about how they developed and managed their farm.

'For heating we use solar and wood,' said Inés, pointing to rows of solar panels. 'We selectively thin the woods on the steep slopes. That's good for the forest and also forms the core of our heating in winter. We recycle our used water through a reed-bed system, and we bottle pure water from the source on the farm.'

'Impressive,' I said. 'I hope we will be as self-sufficient one day.'

'It didn't happen overnight. It has been an ongoing project for more than twenty-five years. And of course, we have new projects every year and trials with new techniques. We keep evolving.'

We reached the house and Inés invited us inside to warm ourselves while she put the dogs back into their run. The fire was blazing. We happily removed a few layers and revelled in the heat.

Guillaume burst through the kitchen door as Inés came in to join us.

'So, what treasure did you unearth?' he asked.

'A little,' said Inés, lifting the pail of truffles.

'*Ah oui*, enough for supper tonight, I think,' Guillaume said and laughed. 'Have a seat and relax by the fire.'

We threw ourselves into the chairs around the table and allowed the warmth to infuse.

'Take your time. We'll be preparing the dinner. We look forward to seeing you at seven p.m.,' said Guillaume, making to leave.

'Before you go, Guillaume, I have a little question. Why no keys for the rooms?' said one madame dripping with jewels – little wonder the question.

'Oh, I have a funny story for you. We stopped using keys because people kept taking them – by mistake *bien sûr*. Our doors are old doors and replacing a lost key is not as easy as a quick trip to the key cutter. We didn't want to lose the character and charm of the place by changing the locks. Anyway, we are so isolated here, the farm is secure, we have dogs, there is no one around but us. So we decided to get rid of the keys. Everything is open – our house, the guest rooms. One day, about five years ago, we had a couple from Paris for the weekend. They looked like they would have been more at home in St Tropez than St Amour. On

Sunday evening the woman came running into reception saying, "My jewels have been stolen!"'

He looked around the room, enjoying the suspense of his story.

'We asked them to look everywhere. They looked again but returned adamant that the jewels, worth about fifty thousand euro, were gone. I called the local police. Half an hour later they arrived. The atmosphere was very strange. We were all potential perpetrators of the crime. With the crisis we weren't able to continue the normal service. Everyone staying at St Amour was gathered together in this room and questioned one by one next door in the parlour by the police, who also searched all the rooms. By midnight we were all exhausted and still there was no sign of the lost jewellery. The couple and the police went back to their room to search one last time. Hidden underneath the Madame's underwear they found her jewels!'

'But it's not possible!' said one of the ladies and clapped her hand over her mouth.

'*Mais oui*. The jewels had been found but we couldn't get the evening back. It was our night of Agatha Christie. We laugh about it now, but I wasn't laughing then. The lesson is: don't hide your jewellery in your underwear.'

He went out laughing heartily, while we, sharing in the laughter, dispersed to our respective rooms.

Sean and I decided to walk the route we had taken to the plateau to see the enchanting truffle fields again. This time we took the longer road back, one that extended further into the new truffle tree section. The air was icy, and it was dark by the time we returned.

To recuperate I lounged in a lavish bath filled with organic bubbles, one of the bathroom treats provided. I felt like a queen. While I soaked, Sean read the newspaper, appreciating the comfortable sofa. It was pure luxury.

After drying myself in a soft-as-down bath sheet, I slipped on a gold G-string – as close as I was getting to jewellery in my underwear. Then I added sheer dark stockings, a little black dress, leather boots and lipstick. I was ready and Sean hadn't even hit the shower.

We exchanged places. I sat reading, enjoying the moment of peace, as I sipped a glass of our *Grâce* red wine that Sean had poured for me.

I felt in a state of grace, grateful beyond measure for this long overdue interlude. Sean emerged from the bathroom dressed in beige chinos and a blue collared shirt that matched his eyes. His golden mane was brushed, tamed into a wavy halo, and his cheeks were shaved – rare in winter, when he needed hair to protect him from the cold while he was out pruning. I almost didn't recognise him. He looked younger without a beard.

'You shine up well,' I said, rising from the sofa. He smiled and opened the door for me.

The dining room had the perfect ambience of low lighting and intimate chatter. We greeted our truffling friends with a '*bonsoir*' and a wave. Inés had changed from farming gear, jeans and a cowboy hat to stockings, miniskirt, and high heels. She showed us to our table and returned with a wine list.

As Sean perused the list and my hands itched to get hold of it, Inés explained quietly that the others were on the seven-course truffle menu, and so that we could keep pace with them, they would offer us a few extra truffle surprises. It was our lucky night. I had gone from no truffle to full-blown truffle in a couple of hours. If the aphrodisiac promise was for real, the place would be steaming.

Inés was welcoming but it was so long since we had dined at an upmarket restaurant that we felt out of place. She returned with a tiny square of lard for each of us, home-made bread, and the aperitif Sean had ordered.

'The idea is to eat the lard on its own. It's to show that a simple product like this, when well raised, is delicious. It also gives you appetite. The bread is made from our own wheat, sea salt, water from our source, and our own living yeast.'

'Thanks, Inés. That looks delicious,' I said, referring to the bread rather than the lard. You couldn't get more local than that: grown, ground and baked on the farm. The lard on the other hand didn't sound gourmet to me. It was a strange start.

'What do you recommend for the wine?' asked Sean. 'We would prefer local and organic.'

'Unfortunately the ones from Cahors are not certified organic,' said Inés. 'We prefer organic and biodynamic wines but in the local selection we don't always have them.'

Sean made his selection of a Cahors from the list and Inés left us. I was disappointed that this icon of organic and biodynamic farming was not selecting organic wines. It didn't make sense. Feeling reticent, I tasted the lard. It was full flavoured and nutty; my preconception was proved incorrect. The bottle of wine arrived accompanied by a side plate of *jambon de porc noir*, ham from black pigs of Gascony home-cured for 24 months.

'These black pigs cannot be raised in intensive conditions. They need to be free to range, ideally in the forest eating acorns and having fun,' Inés explained.

She left and we began to chat about the day: the truffles, the dogs, the freedom we felt in this isolated place, the ideas it sparked.

The menu followed like a symphony. To start, a *velouté du curé*, a velvet-smooth, pastor's soup, made of *potimarron,* a gourd-like, bright orange pumpkin, laced with truffle and a hint of foie gras. The flavours were divine, fit for a priest as the name suggested; I felt like singing hallelujah. There was more truffle in it than had been in the jar I bought for a king's ransom years before. I sipped the Cahors, appreciating the dense dark fruit and tannin, then took my last scoop of soup and sighed. How could things get any better?

But there was more – *bien sûr*. Next was *risotto à la truffe* – home-grown wheat cooked risotto-style with truffle and leeks. The 'simple' dish had depth of flavour and truffle fragrance that filled the stomach and the soul. Soon, the aroma of brioche turned our heads as it came through the door. Each tiny savoury brioche had its own whole truffle inside. We ate slowly, savouring each bite. The infusion of truffle through the soft bread was extreme. Sean was smitten.

At that point our neighbours were served a layered potato dish, a *dauphinoise à la truffe*. It was the only part of the seven-course truffle menu we weren't served and provided a welcome pause.

'That soup and risotto were exceptional,' I said. 'It's the combination of the quality of ingredients and their heritage, the raising of it, and all the steps in the transformation. All three were *juste*. They respect the product through the entire process from the growing to the processing to the final cooking. It's simply perfection and perfect simplicity at once.'

'I wonder if truffles would grow at Garrigue?' mused Sean. A truffle field had become a necessity since tasting the brioche.

Garrigue was the old farm name and also the sector name of our part of the commune of Saussignac. We had changed the farm name to Château Feely, our family name, a few years before because there were so many Garrigue wines on the market already.

'The limestone of their plateau looks like ours,' I replied.

'Hmm, perhaps Dora could become a truffle dog,' said Sean.

'He he. Maybe. But Inés said it took fifteen years for the trees to start giving truffles,' I said. 'I'm not sure our loving Dora will be around for that.'

'But if you're lucky you might get them after five,' said Sean.

'*Exceptionnellement.*'

Sean looked longingly at his empty glass.

'Wine and truffles – they just go together.'

'Absolutely. One for us to look into a little more.'

Inés served the main, *filet mignon de porc aux truffes*, pork tenderloin stuffed with truffle and served with truffle reduction sauce. Sean ordered a glass of another local red.

When it arrived, he took a deep sniff.

'Dark berries, a hint of truffle,' he said. 'This could be a perfect match.'

He took a bite of the pork and truffle sauce and a sip of wine.

'Delicious.'

'I'm jealous,' I said. 'One little sip?'

'No way, you'll leave lipstick on my glass and the wine won't be the same. Petrochemicals.'

Sean was a Luddite when it came to cosmetics.

'No petrochemicals, only natural products,' I said.

'How do you mean natural products? All lipsticks are petrochemical.'

'Not this one,' I said and whipped it out of my bag.

I had converted to organic and natural products, including my lipstick, but even those Sean didn't like. Perfumes and deodorants weren't allowed in our house, only a natural deodorant – and even that wasn't allowed in our bedroom because it brought on a sneezing fit for Sean.

Reluctantly, he passed the wine glass over, and I took a sip. It was softer than the bottle we had ordered but with a good body, dark colour, and black fruit, typical of Cahors Malbec.

'I think what they are doing is inspirational,' I said. 'Products grown on the farm, transformation of products like the ham made with their ancient methods, the restaurant that highlights their own produce. It's a circle like the one we have with the visits, the wines, and the accommodation.'

'Hmm. The idea of a restaurant showcasing the farm's products is good, but I don't like the hours a restaurant requires. We don't have much spare time anyway.'

'True,' I said.

'We need to work smarter,' said Sean.

We were talking about work again. It was inevitable when our lives took place at our work, and we worked together. It was an upside and a downside. We loved what we did and were passionate about it – something that was a luxury in itself.

Inés removed our empty plates and soon returned with *pomme à la truffe*, apple in a rich egg custard laced with truffle. I ate the fruit and left the custard – a step too far for me.

'I love the isolation of this place,' said Sean.

I understood what he meant. Saussignac, our village, and the valley below us were constantly expanding with new houses. The main road beneath the farm had little traffic when we arrived but now carried what seemed to us like a constant stream at peak hours. That said guests always commented on how quiet the farm was. Perhaps we were oversensitive.

'It seems wilder, less chemical farms,' he added.

We were fortunate that most of our vineyard borders were with other organic farmers, like our neighbour Olivier. But when a chemical farmer sprayed, even miles away, we could smell it. The products were not innocent, and they didn't stay on the targeted area. Looking down at the area around Mardenne we would sometimes see plumes of spray drifting well beyond where the sprayer was operating, to neighbouring farms and into the Dordogne River. I had read that 92 percent of France's waterways and rivers were polluted with pesticides from agriculture.

'It looks less intensively farmed here but I bet they have the same problems,' I said.

'But their farm is much bigger. Their buffer areas are larger than ours.'

'We couldn't cope with more land,' I said. 'And anyway, I'm not moving.'

Sean laughed. He knew that I wanted to be buried on our farm. I had always felt a need for an anchor, a root, and I wanted that for me and my family. I loved the solidity, the settledness, of a farm and a family's shared place. I wanted our daughters to know they had a place to come back to when they flew the nest, that there was this solid base in the world. Sometimes the weight of the responsibility of that solid base made me feel like running away. Sometimes it didn't feel that solid, but it was there.

Inés reappeared with a tiny rectangle of chocolate *à la truffe* that signalled the end of the night's feast. It was delicious and heavily laced with black gold. The quantity of wine and food we consumed that night should have sent us straight to sleep. But it didn't. I can confirm the aphrodisiac effect of truffles.

⤜⤜⤜ ⤛⤛⤛

In the morning I woke with the energy of a young lover. Sean was still asleep, so I pulled on my boots for a walk instead. The dawn was breaking, and I had the world to myself. Even the dogs didn't stir as I tiptoed across the courtyard, let myself quietly out of the gate and took the path up to the truffle forest. As I stepped on to the open plateau, snow began to fall, soft white flakes lit up like a silver shower in the light of the dawn rising to the east. Over the white stones and perfectly manicured truffle trees it was like something out of Narnia, a magic land.

I kept walking, pleased to have insulated boots and barely able to believe the beauty. With the snow, the silence was intensified, my footsteps soft in the white blanket forming around me. Clouds sprinkled flakes shimmering silver and gold in the dawn light. I reached the point where we had turned down with Inés and considered going further, to where Sean and I had been the night before. I kept walking. The trees stretched out ahead of me in the swirling flakes. At the next corner I stopped and looked back, hesitating about whether to turn back.

Under the trees the *brûlés* had less snow, their limestone circles a creamy colour against the pure white, punctured every now and then with grass stubble. Beyond the plateau the land plunged away to the valley floor and layers of hills disappeared into distance, folds of lemon, gold and amber. The light and depth created between the snow, the clouds and the rising sun were like a fantasy film. I stayed there, taking in the magic, until the cold in the tips of my fingers drove me home. I thought better of the long route. If the snow was building Sean might want to get home sooner rather than later to avoid Burgundy take two. I teetered down the steep shortcut – even more treacherous with the snow – then stepped it out back to the farmhouse via the lower road.

Sean was up and had packed the car. As expected, he wanted to hit the trail before the snow worsened. Even without snow we had decided that the truffle egg breakfast, while tempting, was beyond our bellies and budget. Besides, another dose of that hefty aphrodisiac could have been dangerous.

We found Inés in the main house.

'I hope you enjoyed it,' she said.

'Oh yes,' I replied. 'Especially hearing about the truffles on our walk with you and the dinner. We're organic and biodynamic farmers. In fact, we brought a gift of two bottles of our wine.'

'That is very interesting and kind,' said Inés. 'Let me see if Guillaume has a moment to talk to you before we serve the breakfast.'

Minutes later we were ushered into the cocoon of their professional kitchen. Their youngest child descended the stairs wrapped in pyjamas and gown. She looked sleepy, like she needed a quiet Sunday with her parents. It was their home as well as their workplace. We knew the feeling. I felt like we were invading their private space, but Guillaume drew us in.

'Come, come,' he said. 'Tell me a little about yourselves. Can I get you a coffee?'

'I would love an espresso,' I said, the idea of a shot before our long drive was tempting.

Sean declined. He had been off caffeinated drinks for years and I guessed was also sensitive to our hosts' right to family time on Sunday.

We took turns to share our story and why the triskell, a three-way spiral, in a mosaic form, was the logo on our label.

'The triskell is an ancient Celtic sign. You can see it carved into rocks at Newgrange in Ireland, a site dating to 3500 BC,' said Sean. 'It's a nod to our Irish roots but we grew up in South Africa. My grandparents that came from Ireland farmed a vineyard in the Cape.'

'Springboks!' exclaimed Guillaume and lifted his jacket to show us a Springbok logo on his shirt.

A look of complicity passed between him and Sean.

Guillaume served me a tiny cup of espresso. Inés took a jug of cream from the fridge and placed it on the counter. I mouthed *merci* so as not to interrupt Sean.

'We thought we would go wine-farming in South Africa, but we moved to Dublin and then we fell in love with French wine on a vineyard holiday to France. It took years to find our farm in Saussignac. We have great *terroir*, a section of limestone plateau similar to yours but smaller.'

'Interesting,' said Guillaume, lifting the bottle for a closer look at the triskell.

'We're passionate about organic and biodynamic farming,' I added. 'The triskell symbolises the biodynamics since the spiral is emblematic of nature and of dynamisation. We're excited and inspired by what you're doing here, your self-sufficiency, the truffles, the food you served last night. It's an experience we'll never forget.'

'Thank you,' he said.

'I have one question,' said Sean. 'How did you make the truffle risotto?'

'Ha ha, you need a lot of truffles,' replied Guillaume and opened the fridge to show us a bowl of dry spelt grains with several large nuggets of fresh truffle nestling inside. 'It is a good way to store the truffles and it gives truffle flavour to the grain.'

'Thank *you* for a fantastic stay,' I said. 'And Inés for the truffling – the afternoon was *magnifique*.'

'Thank you for the wine,' said Guillaume.

We left them to serve breakfast. The retired Parisians were limbering up to start their truffle egg feast. We left feeling a little envious, with the extravaganza of the previous night a strong cerebral and corporeal memory.

Leaving our wine with them felt exposed. I wondered if they would like them. A friend in St-Émilion, Vince Lignac, often said, 'I make the wine I like. I can't please everyone, so I make the wine that reflects my *terroir* – a true wine, not a wine for a market.' That was what we did. The fact that we sold out was a sign that the wine was good. But I still had momentary lapses of confidence in our wines. Like Bo Barrett in the film *Bottle Shock*, when he gives up on his Chardonnay that eventually wins the Judgement of Paris, I hadn't learned to trust them completely.

Whatever about confidence, I had to get on and make wine sales. The *gîte* bookings were slow. I kept getting requests for a swimming pool and a television. We had decided not to install TV, wanting the experience for our guests to be about wine, nature and outdoors. In the early days, with our precarious finances, a swimming pool had been out of the question. A quick online review of competing *gîtes* showed that we had to have one if we wanted our accommodation to be successful. That, and the rising summer temperatures of recent years, made it a necessity.

The getaway had been good for our relationship. But we returned to our bad habits. Sean barely acknowledged my presence when he came through in the morning. I got a grunt rather than a hello or a kiss. My concern about our relationship compounded my sleepless nights. I woke up at 3 a.m. and started writing my second book. I had to make something positive out of the situation.

CHAPTER 4

Orange Eggs

Sean stomped into the kitchen, back after four hours of pruning. I was oblivious to the time, wrapped up in front of my computer working on the final edit of *Grape Expectations*, my first book, due out that summer.

'Where's lunch?' he shouted. 'I'm starving!'

He was frozen and exhausted.

'I didn't notice the time,' I said.

'Yeah, yeah, sitting toasty in the warm house. Couldn't even be bothered to make a hot soup for her husband.'

I unbent myself from the keyboard and pushed back the old wicker chair that had travelled from South Africa with us decades before. Its feet scraped across the wooden floor. I needed a proper desk chair with support and wheels – for my back and for the floor. I hobbled from the 'office', a room in our house, through a dark landing and into our small galley kitchen. After being hunched over the computer for so long I felt stiff as a board.

We dreamed of renovating our house. Since the St Amour truffle getaway, we were crackling with ideas of how to broaden our farming base; thoughts of truffle trees, farm animals and how to take our tourism offer to the next level. Years of investment and effort were required for these initiatives, all of which would take priority over our home renovations.

'Sorry,' I said as I entered the kitchen. Sean's disgust that I didn't turn out a fine farmer's lunch every day was an ongoing tussle with a pinch of joking and a tablespoon of serious.

'Guess I'll make it myself,' he said, putting a handful of just-picked wild leeks and kale on the counter. 'What's wrong with you?'

'Nothing. Just a bit stiff,' I said. 'Should have taken some breaks to stretch but I was so engrossed I didn't.'

'Every hour, Caro. You have to get up and stretch every hour. Or come and do some vineyard work – that would be even better.'

He stepped back on to the porch to take off his boots, put on his house clogs then washed his hands. He turned from the sink and took two homegrown onions from the vegetable rack, a thick wood board and the Henckels knife my sister had given us years before, then returned to the counter nearest the oven.

He chopped like a pro. His right hand took a bit of leftover butter and threw it into the iron pan, warmed by the gas flame. When the butter sizzled, the chopped onions went in, then the wild leeks, followed by kale, and a handful of organic mushrooms, that had been sitting at the back of the fridge. Cooked potatoes from a few nights before were chopped and followed the rest.

'Won't you grab a handful of parsley for me?' he said.
'Sure.'

As I stepped out into the courtyard the cold wind
smacked my face. It felt good, fresh, and alive. I needed
to get out. I missed the outdoors when I was stuck inside
doing administration or writing for days on end. The mass
of parsley that Sean had planted in an old cut-out *barrique*
was in good shape. Second-hand barrels made perfect plant
troughs cut in half or laid sideways with a window cut out
of the top like this one. The parsley was cold and damp
to the touch. I lifted it to my nose and sniffed deeply. It
mingled with the aroma of Sean's cooking wafting on the
air, getting stronger with each step back to the house. My
mouth started to water.

I rinsed the parsley and passed it to Sean. In a flash
it was finely chopped like I could never do. Sean was a
perfectionist chef. He chopped fine. I chopped rough. He
threw the parsley in then piled two stacks of the mix on to
our plates and popped them in the oven.

He placed two of Blanchette's eggs into the pan
alongside two eggs bought from the supermarket to
supplement our now tiny supply. We had kept laying hens
for years but only one, Blanchette, was left of the original
batch of eight. Our homegrown egg supply had been a key
part of our self-sufficiency. In old age, Blanchette still laid
the odd egg, but not enough for our family of four. The
shop ones were a light yellow and Blanchette's were dark
yellow, almost orange. Sean took the plates out of the oven
and placed one of each on top of the mix. The aroma was
savoury and delicious.

'Thanks, Sean,' I said and took the plate. I sat down at
my end of the old pine table and Sean settled into his end.

grass is growing gangbusters, I'll still need the mower since the sheep would eat the young shoots.'

'*Alors* you'd better find out how much the mower will be, and we'll have to build it into the budget.'

'And you had better make sure you find the right eggs.'

'Ecologically it makes total sense to get sheep,' I said. 'I met a couple at the Vinexpo Expression Bio Show last year. They've successfully run sheep on their vines for years. I'll contact them to ask if we can visit.'

Our lunch had been a working lunch again. That afternoon I called Andrea and Fearn, winegrowers and shepherds near Castillon, and re-introduced myself.

'You must come soon so your daughters can see the lambs,' said Andrea. 'Why don't you visit us on Wednesday afternoon? We can show you the sheep and then have afternoon tea.'

I felt Andrea's warmth and open spirit over the phone.

'Thanks, Andrea. That would be perfect,' I said.

We chatted a little about the season before I hung up, delighted to have the sheep research visit lined up.

Wednesdays were half days for schools in France. French school had gone from a four-and-a-half-day week with Wednesday off and a half day on Saturday to the half day on Wednesday then to a four-day week to save money on school transport and then back to the half day Wednesdays when the state realised the teachers couldn't fit all the work into a four-day week. We had barely got used to one programme when it changed again. Each time the days were changed, or the order was switched, the teachers' unions would call for a day of strike action and no one would go to school.

❦

'Wait for us, Mum,' said Sophia.

She and Ellie were a few steps behind me on the library stairs. I stopped and waited for them to catch up.

Sean had started a Saturday routine of library and market in Bergerac, a working town with a beautiful historic medieval centre, twenty minutes from Saussignac. In season, I had *gîte* changeovers and tour clients on Saturdays; now, in winter, I had time while Sean had to be out pruning on all the good-weather days. Some days, like today, the expedition would stretch to include a cream tea at the Victoria Café, offering a touch of glamour to the outing.

From the library we followed the main street to the market, where we would find our artisan organic egg producer and other favourites. The eggs had dark yellow yolks and a taste that told us the chickens were outside eating grass and insects, not only grains. It was not merely the taste that was affected: eggs from outdoor 'grazing' chickens had up to twice as much vitamin E, 40 percent more vitamin A and three times as many omega-3s. Our egg mission addressed both health and taste.

The winter sun's cool rays played across the streets packed with stalls, light and shade changing with the constant movement. People's breath rose like smoke in the air. Sometimes an unknown salesman would take up prime position in front of the church. That day the product was a plastic kitchen utensil and the presenter had a large crowd looking on as he played out his routine. He promised that his gadget would transform your life. It seemed so out of place. I felt like chasing him out of town.

We had learned to buy equipment that would last our lifetimes, if not generations; iron pans, solid metal graters with no plastic attachments. We knew the real thing, like a metal pan or a cast-iron pot, was good value if you considered the lifetime value rather than the one-time cost. My most recent dustpan purchases were metal. Already they had lasted longer than any of the plastic ones in my past. The price was 25 percent more than the plastic version and I had already recouped that in longevity.

We found a passage through the crowd growing around the salesman and I led the way down the side street to the left the church. Our first stop was our organic baker, a shy man. I had bought from him many times but never struck up a conversation. With the church towering above us, we stocked up on wholegrain bread and perfumed chocolate brioche buns for Ellie and Sophia, ending the transaction with a quiet 'thank you'. With bread and brioche safely stored in our cloth shopping bag, we took off again. I found pleasure and satisfaction shopping on the market and getting to know our suppliers. Here a person's product was an extension of themselves. Like us, their products reflected their personalities.

'Wait for us,' shouted Sophia a few steps behind me. 'You're going too fast, Mum.'

I stopped and hung the bag over my shoulder so I could take their hands, gave them both a squeeze and slowed down the pace. Usually I was in such a hurry I raced around the market circuit like it was a F1 track. I had to slow down, to take in the environment with all my senses.

I became aware of smells as I passed different stalls the pungent freshness of the vegetable stands and the rich yeasty aroma of the *boulangers*, of the conversation between market goers and stallholders, of the cooing of the pigeons on the church above us. I looked at the market more closely, as if seeing the patchwork of colours and movement for the first time.

There were large stands packed with masses of produce, traders rather than producers. There were farmers' stands, sometimes two generations or even three, working side by side. At one stand, a couple, weathered and well into their seventies, sat behind a wooden table garnished with plastic containers of walnuts and mushrooms. Behind the containers were a few jars of honey and home-made jam. I wondered how much change they had seen in this town and market in their lifetimes. I was tempted to stop but a quick look at my watch told me that if we wanted to get to the Victoria Café before the lunch rush we had to keep moving.

On the lane that hugged the other side of the church I found Valérie, a natural organic cheese and yoghurt producer that created *tarin*, an unpasteurised cow's-milk cheese that came in small and large rounds and in bricks. It was creamy and delicate, and we loved it. We joined the queue. The tall grey-haired man in front of me ordered his cheese.

'I like your cheese, so I buy it, but I don't see the difference between organic and not organic when it comes to dairy,' he said to Valérie. 'I don't see why I should pay more for organic milk. Aren't they all out eating grass?'

Valérie took a deep breath and a dose of internal patience. She reached for the cheeses he had requested and started to wrap them. Once composed, she looked up and gave him a little smile.

'Well, Monsieur, a few things are different. With conventional you could be drinking milk laced with wormicide, antibiotics and weedkiller, to take a few. Organic dairy means no herbicides, no pesticides, no genetically modified feed, and no antibiotics in your milk. They can be part of your daily dose if you consume conventional dairy.'

'I never thought of that,' he said.

'*Beh oui*, Monsieur. There are many differences. To get back to what you said about the grass, conventional dairy cows can be fed grain indoors for part or all of their lives so they may not be eating grass at all, whereas with organic dairy pasture-fed is guaranteed. And of course, the organic rules mean better care and better health for the cows. I could talk for a long time on this, but I must serve Madame. Thank you in any case.'

He looked like he could have uttered the French term '*bouche bée*', 'mouth wide open', as he took his order off the counter. I felt like running round and giving Valérie a pat on the back, but my daughters found me embarrassing enough so I gave her a wide smile, ordered my cheese and yoghurt, and quietly moved on to make space for the next person.

Valérie probably had stats at her fingertips like I had for wine, including studies showing that artisan organic milk like hers had up to 50 percent more vitamin E, 75 percent more beta-carotene and 70 percent more omega-3 fatty acids than conventional milk. It also had more than double the amount of certain antioxidants, like those that keep your eyes healthy as you age. It wasn't only that you weren't getting the bad things like wormicide, herbicide, and antibiotics; you were getting a product naturally packed with good things.

The number of organic stalls had grown over the years, but it was still relatively low. Based on a quick stall count I estimated less than five percent. For the average person there was a lack of awareness of what organic meant and why it was worth seeking it out, as this man had illustrated. As producers we knew why so deeply that we only ate organic food. We knew that our health was too precious to compromise on what went into our bodies. We didn't have the latest mobile phone and we shared one old car, but we only ate organic.

A few stalls on was our egg producer. I still didn't know her name, but I could tell she recognised my face. She and her partner also grew organic vegetables and produced home-made pasta, including one that was a delightful shade of green thanks to a dose of stinging nettles. It tasted so good – with salad and a little olive oil and garlic, it was a meal in itself.

Stinging nettle is a plant we used in biodynamics. The Latin name of 'nettle' is *urtica*, from *urere*, to burn or scorch, because of how it burns or stings when you touch it. We had masses of it on the farm. I love nettle soup. We also dried the leaves to use as a tea for the vines. Sprayed on the leaves it acts as a mild antifungal. Macerated fresh, the leaves can be used as a fertiliser or a compost spray. The leaves are high in nitrogen and contain magnesium, sulphur, and iron, thus are a good compost activator too.

Loaded with our shopping, bulked up with stinging-nettle pasta and eggs, we walked down the cobbled streets of old Bergerac to the pedestrianised lane that held the Victoria. An olde English-style metal sign hanging on a gold chain announced the café, wedged in above the tea shop. The French couple that ran it were tea fanatics.

Inside, the cramped space was like a *Harry Potter* film set except that instead of magic sweets or sorcery books there was tea and every type of tea accessory you could imagine. The wooden beams were hung with hooks carrying mugs; the walls were lined with shelves crammed to bursting with teacups, pots, caddies, and related decor. Display cabinets filled the floor space save for a skinny corridor that passed by the sales counter and went up a steep set of wooden stairs to the cosy teahouse. Deep armchairs and tea tables lined the outer walls, and bistro-style tables and chairs filled the middle. The walls were hung with English-style memorabilia of horses, rugby and gardening. Ellie and Sophia made for the armchairs closest to the window.

'Luxury!' I said, taking the bistro chair that was left.

'*On est bien la, hnn,*' said Ellie, looking smug and sounding so French.

Monsieur Victoria appeared and handed us the menus. 'On special today we have tiramisu and black forest cake.'

'It is a special day *alors*,' I said. 'Sophia and Ellie love tiramisu.'

'Hot chocolate and tiramisu please,' said Sophia.

'The same,' said Ellie.

'Please,' I said.

'Please,' added Ellie.

'Organic Earl Grey tea and scones for me please,' I said.

Monsieur Victoria thanked us and whisked himself away, swishing behind the pink cotton curtain that marked the entrance to the galley kitchen where they worked their wonders.

I tried to inculcate in my daughters how important it was to say 'please' and 'thank you' and to take time to be grateful each day, but sometimes it felt like a losing battle.

'I'll have to give you punishment like I had at boarding school,' I said. 'Early rising. That was getting up at five thirty to do an hour of hardcore exercise before the school day. We had to run so much that some kids would vomit. We were so stiff the following day we could barely walk up the stairs.'

'Ha ha,' said Ellie.

'You laugh. But if you don't remember to be *gentille* then I'll have to start doing that. There'll be a double benefit because you won't forget your manners and you'll get fit.'

'Oh, Mum, that was of your days. Of our days we don't do things like that,' said Sophia, using her own special English expression 'that was of your days' based on the French '*de nos jours*'.

'But wc should,' I said, barrelling ahead. 'And I think we need a six-day week like we had – a full work week with a half day on Saturday. None of this four-day week nonsense.'

A look of horror spread across their faces. I burst out laughing and they did too.

Monsieur Victoria swooshed back to our table with a tray loaded with goodies.

'A hot chocolate and tiramisu for mademoiselle, a hot chocolate and tiramisu for the other mademoiselle and the Earl Grey and scone for Madame.'

'Thank you,' I said.

'Thank you,' chimed Sophia and Ellie, clearly frightened by the threat of early rising.

'*C'est moi. Bon appetit*,' he said.

The term '*c'est moi*' directly translated as 'it's me', a short way of saying 'it's me that thanks you'.

I took a sip of Earl Grey and a bite of my scone with jam and cream. I was not like many of my daughters' friends' mums, who were into clothes, make-up, city living and things like shopping. I was into walking, farming, wine, and the outdoors. I had to find things for us to enjoy together without doing what I didn't like or what they didn't like. Before we knew it, they would be grown up.

'Yum,' I said and took another bite of scone loaded with jam and cream.

'You have cream just there,' said Sophia, pointing to a glob of cream on my top lip.

'Thanks,' I said, wiping it away. 'Thinking of school days, wouldn't it be great to go to South Africa?'

'Oh yes!' said Sophia.

'So good,' said Ellie.

'So long as there's no "early rising" there,' said Sophia. She frowned then laughed.

'When can we go?' asked Ellie.

'It depends on how quickly we can save enough money,' I said. 'We'll have to work towards it. It means saving our money instead of going shopping and having fancy cream teas.'

They looked crestfallen.

'It'll be worth it,' I promised.

It was 12 years since I had been back to South Africa, the land of the first 27 years of my life. Sophia and Ellie had never visited it. We had been so focused on our farm that a trip had not entered my head. Now, as I thought about it, I felt a wave of homesickness, of missing South Africa, a feeling I had kept at bay by necessity. I added the cost of flights to my list of budget priorities. For the balance of our lives, for our daughters to know their roots, to see Sean's parents, for so many reasons, we had to go.

≫≫ ≪≪

We had become a Demeter certified biodynamic farm and with that certification came the obligation to have animals. Demeter is the largest biodynamic certification body in the world. They ensure that products that carry their logo and the 'certified biodynamic' label meet the rigorous standards of biodynamic farming and production. We knew we would continue to keep chickens but not as free as they had been. A reckless chicken had trashed the tasting-room table the previous year, smashing glasses and creating mayhem. They were so friendly they left their manure gifts near the front door and on the terraces of the *gîtes* and the tasting room. A wine-tasting experience that included the stink of chicken poo was not one that we wanted. We had to rethink our chickens.

If we couldn't control a few chickens, considering more animals didn't seem like a great idea but it didn't stop us visiting Château Brandeau, the vineyard in Castillon. They had been mowing their vines with sheep for decades. I loved the idea of a closed circuit where the sheep ate the grass and returned the manure to the fields as they browsed – and gave us meat in the process. But we were frightened by the extra responsibility and bureaucracy animals would bring. Already it was difficult to get away. If we had farm animals, it would be even more so.

Château Brandeau was in a valley bowl nestled against the plateau of Castillon. The final stretch up to the farm was a swathe of rolling hills filled with vines and patches of forest. In the gravelled entrance a black *deux chevaux Citroën* added a touch of French cachet to the natural beauty. Alongside the parking area a lean-to shed packed with farming equipment rested on a limestone cliff, and on the opposite side an old farmhouse with climbing roses and a brand-new winery smacked contrasting facades uncomfortably together.

A tall solid man with shoulder-length white hair stepped out of the front door and crossed the gravel.

'Fearn,' he said, stretching out his hand.

'Andrea,' said the wiry, strawberry blonde woman, that was a few steps behind him.

'Caro, *enchanté*,' I responded, shaking hands, and introducing our family. 'Thank you for inviting us. Your farm is beautiful.'

'It's home,' said Andrea. 'Perhaps we should start outside and then visit the new winery before we have tea.'

She looked dubiously at our footwear. 'I have some spare boots.'

She and Fearn were well shod for the season, sporting serious wellingtons. Sean was the only one on our team with the right equipment; I felt like a right 'townie', the name country kids gave to city kids when I was growing up. Andrea headed inside for extra wellies.

'A fire took out the winery two years ago,' explained Fearn, noticing that we were looking at the modern winery building. 'We were lucky we didn't lose the house, and the insurance paid for this new, better insulated version.'

'How frightening,' I said.

'It was.' A look crossed his face that said he wouldn't enjoy stirring up the memory.

Andrea returned with boots, and we pulled them on. She went back inside and came out again with two wine bottles fitted with teats.

'To feed the lambs,' she said, seeing our questioning looks.

'All ready?' asked Fearn.

We nodded.

'*Alors*, let's go!'

We followed him down the muddy track with Ellie staggering after us in boots five sizes too big.

'You were asking about the administrative part of the livestock,' said Fearn. 'We went the simple route. We keep the sheep to mow the grass but we don't sell the meat. We have to declare them but the administration is relatively light. If we wanted to sell them as organic meat there would be a lot more hoops to jump through.'

'That's what we were worried about,' said Sean.

I left the two men talking and pulled back to help Ellie, who was trailing behind. Andrea drew back too.

'Don't worry, Ellie, it isn't far,' she said. 'You'll see. And it'll be worth it. There are new lambs.'

We passed through a wide farm gate into a vineyard enclosed by brush and forest. I spied the sheep at the top end and pointed them out to Ellie. Some had already seen us and were running down the hill, their long tails flapping. In the group were two black lambs with white faces and a touch of white on their tails.

'I'll show you how to feed them then you can do it yourselves. OK?' said Andrea to Sophia and Ellie.

They were a little scared at first. They had never been this close to sheep before. I felt as if I were in a time warp – growing up, my favourite pet was an orphan lamb called Mini, shortened to Min. She was born premature and at night my grandmother woke up to feed her with an eyedropper every couple of hours. Min made it against the odds. She would hear my voice when I returned home from school and race across the paddocks and cry, '*Maaa maaaaa*' at the gate until I came and let her out to be with me. She was closer to me than my dog.

'They are so cute,' said Sophia as the lamb sucked on the bottle she was holding.

'I want one, Mummy,' said Ellie.

'They are very cute, my kiddies. But if we get sheep, they have to pay for themselves. They would mow the grass and we would eat them.'

'Never!' exclaimed Sophia.

'No way!' added Ellie.

'Well, you do need to find a use for the excess rams and eating them is a good solution,' said Andrea. 'Officially we don't eat ours – they die of natural causes. They're only here to mow the grass and they do it very well.'

Andrea was a wise woman. She didn't talk a lot, and when she did you listened.

'It's getting cold. Would you girls like to see the horses before we go in for tea?' she said.

'Yes please!' replied Sophia and Ellie in unison.

I was pleased to see my lesson in *politesse* at the Victoria Café was paying off.

'Fearn, you show Sean and Caro the new winery and I'll take Sophia and Ellie via the horses,' said Andrea, leading the way back out of the gate. Sophia and Ellie happily followed. Usually they would have been shy of someone they had just met but Andrea was already their friend.

Leaving them with the horses, I caught up with Sean and Fearn in the new winery. It was a dramatic contrast to the rest of the farm. The clinical, square space housed large, stainless steel tanks and an upper level of two drywall offices and a washroom.

'It's easier to keep things clean in this new space,' said Fearn. 'The last vintage was great. Perhaps the best we ever made.'

He moved along and led the way out. We passed from the modern block into the house through a narrow stone passage that seemed as old as time. We popped out into a warm living space with oak beams overhead. The open-plan kitchen, dining and lounge oozed comfort. It was ancient and loved.

Andrea was making tea. Sophia and Ellie sat on a brown sofa next to the wood-fired stove, stroking a cat. I felt like a time traveller. Fearn invited us to sit. I sank into a threadbare chair near the fire. It felt snug as a hug. Andrea cut into a loaf of freshly baked banana bread and the aroma spread through the room, adding another layer of comfort.

Fearn and Sean talked about farming while the girls continued to stroke the cat and I joined Andrea at the well-worn counter.

'When we started nearly thirty years ago, we quickly realised we had to find another income. The farm couldn't support both of us. I ended up teaching to make ends meet.'

'I know the feeling,' I said. 'That's what led us into the tourism activities we offer but for me it was a lifesaver.

After being an IT consultant and project manager, being a lonely farmer's wife in rural Dordogne was a culture shock. The wine school saved my sanity.'

'I can see that,' said Andrea as she passed me a cup of steaming tea and a plate of fragrant bread.

'We did it for necessity, but I love being with people and running workshops. It was a perfect fit,' I said.

'Not like me. I didn't want to teach. I wanted to be in the vineyard. I spend all my spare time with the vines. I love it. I can't wait for next year when I retire so I can be back in the vines full-time.'

'Gosh, Andrea, it seems unfair that you couldn't do that and pursue your passion. It's a tough wine market.'

'Hmm, and it hasn't got any easier. Our costs have gone up every year but the price we are paid has often gone down. I'm thankful I did the teaching so I'm guaranteed a better retirement than a farmer. But I still can't wait to stop and get back to the vines.'

We handed out tea and bread to the others then settled around the fire.

'So, you're going to get some sheep then?' asked Fearn.

'Perhaps in a year or two,' replied Sean. 'I'm not sure we're ready.'

'Just dive in and do it the way we do,' said Andrea.

'You're probably right, Andrea, but we're saving for a dream holiday to South Africa. To make it worthwhile we need to be away at least three weeks. Until we've done that trip, we don't want more animals to worry about... And the trip isn't going to happen tomorrow.'

'I see. Well, it's possible to get an automatic water trough filler and if they're out on pasture in a secure enclosure you could leave them for a couple of days, but not three weeks.

For so long you'll need to get a house-sitter to keep an eye on the place, won't you?'

'Hmm, I hadn't thought of that,' I said, realising that it wasn't just money that needed to be saved for our trip to come to fruition.

When we said our farewells, I felt like we knew Fearn and Andrea well even though we had only shared a couple of hours with them. We felt satisfied: corporeal satisfaction from bellies full of banana bread; 'thinking' satisfaction from another key piece of research for biodiversity on the farm; and, above all, satisfaction of spirit, thanks to the richness of the interaction with this peaceful couple.

❧❧❧ ❦❦❦

'You won't believe it!' shouted Sean that weekend. He was in the lounge and I was in the kitchen. 'There's an article about Brandeau here!'

He was clearing out a trunk of old journals and found an article he had kept from a Canadian smallholder magazine we bought on a trip ten years before. The writer had visited Fearn's parents in the early eighties, then visited Fearn and Andrea 20 years later. He wrote about how, when he first visited, the farms in the locality were small mixed farms. You could buy all your food from local artisans within walking distance of the farm: milk, cheese, bread, honey, vegetables, meat, fruit, and wine *bien sûr*. By his second trip, many farms had consolidated; they were bigger and had specialised in winegrowing. There was no other local food. Now the only food supply was a huge shopping centre a car journey away.

'But we want our week of holiday in Provence. Dora can go to the kennels, but chickens and sheep are another story. And what about South Africa?' asked Sean.

'But we need chickens,' I said, beginning to get irrationally angry.

'I know, Caro, but you know that we don't have a neighbour we can rely on, especially now that Sonia and Fred are moving. We can think about chickens after Provence and then we can think about sheep after South Africa.'

'And another thing,' I said, feeling aggressive and taking off on a different tack. 'We don't talk about anything but business – you don't even say good morning to me. We're no better than people sharing a house. We have to sort it out.'

Sean looked at me wide-eyed and I stormed out like an angry toddler. With my broken nights I was tired and irritable. I felt like I couldn't keep up with the demands being made on me. I wanted to run away, to be free from the incessant work of our growing business.

On the outside people looking in thought we were successful, that things were going so well. On the business front things had turned around. Each month was no longer a precipice like it had been in the early days. But despite the relative financial stability I was so stretched I couldn't appreciate it.

I reminded myself how much I had to be thankful for. We had made it through another harvest and our fruit was safely in the winery. We had a fire to keep us warm in winter, and a garden and food store filled by Sean's green fingers. Despite my reframing I couldn't overcome the darkness that kept creeping over me, a film of depression and insomnia that had appeared out of nowhere, sapping my energy and optimism.

CHAPTER 5

Chance Meetings

The weather turned dark like my mood. It was late spring, time for the vines to set their flowers, and it should have been sunny. We needed the bees buzzing and the kids blowing dandelion fuzz. We should have been running through the light-filled vineyards singing gleefully, 'The vines are alive with the sound of music.' Instead, temperatures plummeted, and it poured with rain. It had been hot, so the vines flowered since they knew they had to follow their seasonal progression but cold and damp wrecked the transformation from flower to fruit.

Like harvest, flowering can be a scary time for a winegrower. Each tiny cream flower has the potential to turn into a grape given the right conditions. The conditions were not right and a toll had been taken but we didn't know the extent of the toll. To know the damage, we had to wait for the bunches to form, but industry experts predicted significant losses.

I consoled myself that my mum and dad's golden wedding anniversary was around the corner. In a few weeks, friends and family from South Africa, Zimbabwe, the UK, USA, and Canada would converge on our farm, a place to meet in the middle. My brother, who I hadn't seen in more than a decade, and his family were coming from British Columbia and my sister from California. I felt a shaft of happiness shine through my dark funk.

Then my brother called to say that they couldn't make it after all. His IT support business had been hit with some nasty surprises that quarter and he needed to be at work. He didn't have anyone to fill in for him on crucial projects. Our children had never met. It had been too long already and now it was going to be even longer. The news added to my grim mood.

Vinexpo, one of the largest wine fairs in the world, took place every two years in Bordeaux, usually just after the flowering. A few years before I had participated in the Expressions Bio, an exclusively organic show that took place at the same time. We rarely participated in wine shows; they were an expense that was hard to justify with the volumes we produced. Now our local organic winegrower association announced that Expressions Bio was being held within the Vinexpo halls and they would cover half the costs. We decided to attend.

Wine shows were a great way to meet other winegrowers, as much an inter-winegrower networking event as they were a selling event. I loved meeting other people that were as passionate about organic wine as I was. It was also a chance to swap wine with those growers and keep our cellar stocked so we didn't get 'cellar palate': a well-known trap that winegrowers could fall into, drinking only their own wine so it became the only one they liked.

I was excited that I was sharing a stand with my friends Clément and Francine Klur from Alsace. Spending two days with them would be like taking a tonic – and I needed one. On the way into the show, I shared a ride with a friend, Thierry, who farmed about five kilometres away from us. The drive into Bordeaux offered a chance to catch up; to talk about everything from the state of the wine market to our business with Naomi Whittel of Reserveage for our dried grape skins. Naomi had contributed to turning our failing farm around a few years before, the story told in *Saving Our Skins*. Instead of the used grapes going to compost or to the government distillery we dried them and sold them to Naomi. She created a resveratrol antioxidant food supplement from our skins and other ingredients, essentially an anti-ageing vitamin supplement. Thierry's relationship skills had developed her initial contact through our website into something enduring. Chatting non-stop, the 90-minute drive felt like 15.

We unpacked Thierry's red *forgon* - utility van - and set up our wines on our respective stands. I had received the first few copies of a Polish translation of my book, *Grape Expectations*, and I laid a copy of the original in English and the Polish one alongside our wines. Having my book translated felt grand, like I had hit the big league.

A few minutes before the show opening, Clément and Francine came flying down the alley, arguing with each other. Their partner rivalry reminded me of Sean and myself. It took a very strong relationship to work together. They pulled in next to me behind our shared table.

'*Caaarrrrooooo, comment va?*' asked Clément, letting go of his wine trolley and hugging me close. Clément was a happy Bacchus with curly brown hair, beard, apple cheeks and a smile that took your cares away. He was always upbeat and ready for a laugh.

Francine drew in behind him, a second wine trolley in hand. She was delicate with long hair and fine features, but beneath the calm-looking exterior was a cauldron of energy and an iron will, like a wise woman plugged into an electric current. Clément was convivial and laid-back while Francine was super organised and dynamic. They made a powerful combination.

'*Très bien!* All the better for seeing you!' I replied as I hugged Francine. It was four years since we had visited their vineyard in Alsace.

Clément took off to fetch another load from the car.

'What was the argument about?' I asked as we unpacked wines.

'Oh, something about how we'll build our new wood house,' replied Francine. 'We're planning to move out so our old house can become apartments. Nothing at all. We were squabbling over nothing. As usual.' She laughed.

'Sounds familiar – just like Sean and I do.'

'Men can be so *têtu*! So stubborn!' said Francine. '*Allez hop!* It doesn't look like I'll have time for a coffee.'

A *caviste*, a wine-shop owner and client of theirs, presented himself at the stand. The show hadn't even officially started, and they already had a client. The Klur stand was always buzzing with action. Their family vineyard had been in business for more than 400 years. It was about the same size as ours but with significantly higher density – that is, more vines per hectare. In addition, the grape types grown in Alsace were more productive than ours. Alsace maximum yields were around 8,000 litres per hectare while for most of Bordeaux and Bergerac standard appellations they were 6,700 litres per hectare. For some commune appellations like Margaux the limit was 4,500 litres per hectare, and for our dessert wine appellation of Saussignac it was 2,500 litres per hectare. With Klur's larger volumes they did business with specialist wine shops and restaurants all over France as well as exporting to many countries. The clients kept pouring through.

'How's the *gîte* business going?' I asked as we chatted during a brief lull.

'Good,' said Francine. 'Last year was a great year. How about you?'

'I lost a few potential clients because they want a swimming pool.'

'We find the same thing. With global warming, clients want a swimming pool, even in Alsace,' said Francine. 'But how to do it ecologically? Last year we created a small dam, like a natural swimming pool, that our guests can use. We've filled it with plants that clean the water, so we don't have to add chemicals.'

'Wow, Francine! You're always a step ahead! I've been looking at natural swimming pools but they're so expensive and they say not to use sunscreen. We can't ask guests to go without sunscreen.'

'Hmm. Yes, it's complicated for that, and for the bureaucracy too,' said Francine.

She explained the bureaucratic hoops they had to jump through for approval and promised to send me details of their installation and links to their suppliers. I was in research mode for a swimming pool and hungry for information.

Another client had arrived and, after pouring for him, Clément offered me a taste of the Klur Gewürztraminer. It was an aroma bomb; an explosion of rose and lychee. I sniffed for a few moments, enjoying the aromas before taking a sip, swirling it around in my mouth for a few seconds and spitting into the spittoon. It was slightly sweet but with a lovely freshness; a brightness that was the signature of biodynamic wines.

'How are the new Lodge and tasting room working out?' asked Francine.

'Great. They're paying for themselves but it's a lot of work. I'm stretched.'

'You need to find a good person to help you.'

'But, Francine, we're so scared of French employment law. It's a minefield.'

'It is. We've had some expensive experiences over the years.'

She went on to describe their stories and those of neighbours and friends. It confirmed what I feared: for a small business one bad hire could be the end.

'You have to be very careful about who you select. It's difficult to find really good people. Try to keep the contract as flexible as possible until you're sure.'

'Thanks, Francine. I really appreciate your advice. What about you? Any new projects?' I asked.

'Of course! Always. We're building a new ecological house as our home – that's what we were arguing about when we arrived. Then our current house will be renovated and rented out like the other apartments.'

'A big project,' I said.

'Yes, with many, many decisions and that means many arguments,' she said and laughed again.

Two gentlemen presented themselves at my side of the stand.

'Excuse me, Francine,' I said.

'*Bonjour, messieurs,*' I said. 'Welcome. I usually start the tasting with our driest white wine, a pure Sauvignon Blanc that we call *Sincérité*. Is starting with the dry whites suitable for you?'

I asked this question because sometimes buyers tasted one specific type of wine at a time.

'*Beh oui,*' said the stockier of the two in an accent of South-West France.

'Château Feely is an organic and biodynamic vineyard based in Saussignac, near Bergerac.' I poured the Sauvignon Blanc then held up the bottle for them to see the label and gave them a moment to taste.

'*Moi j'aime bien*. I like it,' said the other man in English-accented French. '*Et toi, Raymond?* What do you think?'

'Me also, I like it a lot. It's lively,' replied Raymond. 'I like wines like this. Racy.'

'The *Sincérité* is from two small parcels of Sauvignon Blanc, one on the plateau and the other an east-facing vineyard that descends off the plateau. They're middle-aged vines with their roots deep in the limestone. Farming organically and biodynamically on the limestone gives freshness and minerality.'

'I can see what you are saying,' said Raymond.

'Yes, me too,' said the other gentleman, writing in a pocket-sized notebook as he spoke.

'Now a white that is smoother, rounder, richer. *Générosité*, our barrel-aged Semillon,' I said and poured into their outstretched glasses.

Another winegrower from Saussignac, Jean-Marie, waved as he approached my stand.

'Caro, can I interrupt?' he asked.

'*Bien sûr*,' I said.

'Monsieur Walker, please may I have a photo with you?' he said to the gentleman who was writing notes. 'My clients in Germany will be so impressed. I'm an organic winegrower in Saussignac, like Caro, but most of my export business is in Germany.'

'Of course,' said Monsieur Walker. 'Please excuse us for a minute, Madame.'

'Sorry to steal your tasters, Caro,' said Jean-Marie. 'Monsieur Walker is a famous author. His books are bestsellers in Germany.'

They disappeared while I digested the brief introduction. Not only was Monsieur Walker famous, but he and his friend were totally charming. I hoped they would come back and not get caught up somewhere else, as sometimes happened at wine shows.

A few minutes later, I was delighted to see them back at my stand.

'Sorry, we should have introduced ourselves. I'm Martin,' said the famous author. 'This is my friend Raymond.'

'Caro. *Enchanté*.' I reached out to shake Martin's hand then to Raymond to do the same.

He took my hand and kissed it in a gallant gesture. I blushed.

'Thanks for stopping to taste with me,' I said.

'It's our pleasure,' said Martin. 'Especially for lovely wines like this.'

I continued through the range, moving from whites to reds and explaining our story as I went.

'They're beautiful wines, but not only that – they're presented by a beautiful young girl as well,' said Raymond.

'I'm completely in accord with you, Raymond. Magnificent wines and a charming young hostess,' said Martin.

I giggled and blushed like a schoolgirl.

'And she lives not far from us. I think we'll have to visit the vineyard,' said Martin.

'Of course,' said Raymond. 'Next time we are in the Bergerac direction we will visit, if we are welcome.'

'Of course!' I said. 'With great pleasure. Where do you live?'

'Le Bugue,' replied Martin.

'Where is that?'

'Near Trémolat.'

'Oh, Trémolat. I've never been but there's a restaurant there that I would love our wines to be in – it's called Le Vieux Logis.'

'That's one of my favourites. It's a great restaurant and I agree it would be a good place for your wines,' said Martin.

I poured the last in the range, our Saussignac dessert wine.

'This is pure gold,' said Raymond.

'Absolutely,' said Martin.

'It won the gold medal on this show's blind-tasting competition,' I said, pointing to the medal sticker on the bottle.

We didn't usually enter competitions because we didn't have enough volume but this one did not require a minimum volume. Competitions cover some of their costs by selling the medals. It's not that they sell them to the highest bidder; they sell them only to those who legitimately win the blind-tasting competition, but they set minimum volumes because if the winning wine is only 1,000 bottles and not 100,000 then the income from the sale of those medal stickers is significantly lower.

'It won ahead of the other dessert wines, including *grand cru classés* from Sauternes,' I added proudly.

'Just what I said. Gold,' responded Raymond. 'More proof that the Dordogne produces better wine than Gironde.'

'Best-kept secret in France,' added Martin.

We shared a conspiratorial laugh. I gave Martin a copy of *Grape Expectations*, feeling anxious about giving it to a world-famous author. We said farewell and they promised to call in on the farm.

Their visit left me powered up like I had downed a caffeine-packed energy drink, but without the heart palpitations. In the short encounter I felt like I had made two new friends. Perhaps they would visit in the summer as promised. I hoped they would. I didn't have their contact details but I did have Martin's name.

At the end of the show, I said goodbye to Clément and Francine, feeling sad that we couldn't see each other more often. The two days had passed in a blur of exchanges.

'I'll send you the pool info. Call me if you need more advice,' said Francine. 'You need to find someone to help you. Why not take on an apprentice? That could be a good way to start. But, like with all hires, it depends on choosing the right person.'

With that thread thrown out, Francine raced off up the corridor after Clément. Alsace was far, far away. They had a ten-hour journey back to their home in Katzenthal.

That night I looked Martin up. He was famous for a detective series called *Bruno, Chief of Police*, set in the heart of the Dordogne. I downloaded one of his books and couldn't put it down. The story flowed like music; he played the joys of the Dordogne with a dose of the reality of rural life and a touch of thriller into a glorious, fulfilling symphony.

The following day, an email from Martin popped up in my inbox:

"It was a pleasure to meet you yesterday. I was enchanted by *Générosité*, *Sincérité* and *La Source*. Congratulations to you and Sean. But I was also moved and delighted by *Grape Expectations*. There were times I laughed aloud; other times I was almost in tears. It is a splendid book, which says a lot about wine, the passion of winemaking, family life and France. I shall be putting your wines on the recommended list on my website."

He had read my book in one night. His compliments filled me with joy and a recommendation from Martin would bring credibility and more visitors. But could I cope with more visitors? The previous season I had skated along, pulling strings together by good luck as much as good management. Or by good luck and a good husband, according to Sean, who had bailed me out for a double-booking. I hoped I would cope this season.

Spring gave way to summer and with it came the promised, and welcome, streams of visitors. But I felt myself drowning. I was looking forward to my parents' golden wedding anniversary; to seeing them but also to having help from my mum with the lunches, laundry, and non-stop action. But that was a short-term plaster. I needed a longer-term solution.

Francine's recommendation echoed in my head, and I looked up apprenticeship in France. It appeared to be a way to put a toe into the employment market without exposing ourselves to too much risk. I sent emails asking for advice on the subject from our accountant and from Isabelle, our friend Thierry's wife who was a teacher at a local agricultural college. We had to find a way to get to the next level with our growing business that didn't include me having a nervous breakdown and our family tearing apart.

CHAPTER 6

Golden Wedding

'To Lyn and Cliffie!' said Gyles, a tall, elegant Zimbabwean with a ring of white hair circling his bald head. He lifted his glass to toast my mum and dad.

We leaned in and said cheers over the old pine table, ensuring we made eye contact as 'To Lyn and Cliff!' echoed round the room.

'That Champagne is delicious, Caro,' said Rosie, Gyles's wife. 'Can I have some more please?'

Laughter rippled among the people gathered. Rosie was a party girl with a naughty sense of humour. I explained that Feely Brut sparkling *méthode traditionnelle* - traditional method - was made in the same way as Champagne but it wasn't Champagne since we produced it on our organic farm in South-West France. Appellation names are ruthlessly protected in France, and none more so than Champagne.

Soon happy chatter was ringing around the room. The house was filling up. Mum and Dad arrived from Canada, then Aunt Sally from South Africa, and Gyles and Rosie from Zimbabwe. Gyles was best man at my parents' wedding 50 years before and Sally matron of honour.

Gyles and Rosie had visited us before. Over the years they had painted shutters, tied down vines, painted our front door and left their positive mark on the physical place, and on our morale. It was Sally's first visit to our farm; I hadn't seen her in two decades. At three years off 80 she still raced around like a forty-something and had shrugged off the long journey as if she had come from next door. Sally is my mum's aunt but almost the same age. For their first seven years she and Mum grew up like sisters, sharing the house that belonged to my great-grandmother because my grandmother, Gigi, had moved home while my grandfather was away for the Second World War. Sally had taken me under her wing when I moved to Cape Town for my first full-time job, filling me with figs from their garden and helping my transition to a new city. As I looked around the room, I felt gratitude and love for the people gathered.

With toasts complete, Mum and Sally returned to aperitif preparations and I joined them on the other side of the table to cut slices of *saucisson*.

'Did you see Foo's photo of her night in Vancouver?' asked Mum.

'Yes, what a stunning pic,' I said.

Jacquie, my sister, nicknamed Foo, was visiting friends in Canada en route to the celebrations in Saussignac.

'She looks so happy. I can't wait to see her and meet Wade,' I said.

Six months earlier Foo had moved to Palm Springs in California to marry Wade. The Vegas wedding photos showed a gorgeous couple in love. But Wade wasn't in the photo in Vancouver; he was still in Palm Springs and due to join us two days after she arrived.

Mum's tablet rang in the bedroom. She washed her hands and disappeared down the corridor. A minute later I passed her door to fetch plates from our side of the house. Her face was white as a sheet. I felt a stab of fear. Speechless, she held the tablet up and I read the message from Foo.

"Had to miss my flight to London last night and fly back to LA. At 4 p.m. I got a call to say that Wade had been in a serious car accident. He went into surgery last night to set his right leg which is pretty smashed. He is going to be OK but will remain in the hospital for a while. Wade needs me right now. I am not in a state to talk to anyone… Haven't slept. Forgive me for not calling. Sending love, Foo."

'Oh my God,' I said.

Mum had tears in her eyes.

'Don't worry, Mum. Wade will be OK. He's young and fit.'

'I know, darling. I'm sure he will be OK. But I was so looking forward to seeing him and Foo; to being together.'

I wrapped my arms around my mum and hugged her tight, tears welling up in my eyes too.

'I'm so sorry, Mum,' I said.

She felt so fragile. Usually, my mum was a powerhouse. She was tall, beautiful, and strong. Normally she was the one comforting me. Now the roles had reversed. I wished that I could make the bad news go away.

'We'll still have a good time. Look at your wonderful friends that are here to celebrate,' I said, trying to ease the blow.

'I know. But it's our kids that we most want to share this with.'

'I'll have to make up for it.'

Mum gave me a sad smile, tears swimming in her eyes. I pulled her close for another hug.

'Everything will be all right. Like Foo says, everything happens for a reason, even if we don't understand it right now. We have to be strong,' I added, sounding more convinced than I felt.

We sat on the bed for a few moments, my arm tight around my mum.

'I'd better get a grip on myself so I can tell everyone,' she said, and gave me a determined smile.

We went through to the kitchen where the noise level had risen in cadence with the descent in the bottle of Feely sparkling.

'What's wrong, Lyn?' asked Sally.

'Oh, Sal.' Mum paused for a moment, trying to formulate the best way to share the message and keep her composure. 'Wade has had a bad car accident and Foo has had to go back to Palm Springs. He's OK but neither of them is going to get here.'

'Hell,' said Dad, overhearing and taking the tablet Mum passed over so he could read the message.

'Oh, Lyn,' said Sally, giving Mum a hug.

'What a bugger-up,' said Dad.

Dad's reaction was anger and frustration while Mum's was sadness. Whenever an accident happened growing up, Dad would get mad. Instead of comforting us he got angry about how we had let the accident happen. He wanted to work out how we could avoid the same thing happening in the future. He had worked hard to provide for us, to ensure we didn't have a precarious childhood like he had. Dad had integrity and grit, but he was strict and didn't like uncertainty or problems that could have been avoided. In our family I sometimes reacted the same way; I knew it was something I had to control.

'I'm so sorry, Lyn,' said Gyles.

The room was quiet for a few moments then Rosie grabbed her champagne flute.

'Well, that means more Champagne for us! Oops, I mean sparkling,' she said, lifting her glass and catching my eye. 'I have to say, it is rather lovely. One of the best I've ever had. May I have a little more please?'

'*Bien sûr*, Rosie!' I said. 'We never run out of wine here. We couldn't drink all the wine we have on the property.'

'We'll have a good try,' said Gyles, holding out his glass.

I did a tour of the room to refill.

'I'm still amazed at how you hooked such a good-looking and smart girl, Cliffie,' said Gyles.

Mum gave a smile as everyone laughed. There was constant banter between Dad and Gyles. With Gyles, Rosie and Sally on-site, my parents wouldn't be down for long. More friends were due to arrive the following day. Even without my sister and brother we would be a good crowd. That didn't take away the sadness I felt that they would not be with us or the worry about Wade.

The next day Foo messaged that Wade was recovering well. At least concern about his health would not hang over the celebration. Her message was upbeat. We had no idea of the trauma she was going through on the other side of the Atlantic. The accident had taken a very serious turn as one of the passengers in the other car had died. It was not only Wade's health Foo was worried about but the wider implications of the accident on their lives.

Oblivious to that, my thoughts were consumed with decisions about food. What, how much, when, who? More friends had arrived hence there were more people to feed. I sent Mum and Sally into the garden to forage for vegetables and set a pot of basmati rice to cook.

Sally and Mum rounded up a team of sous-chefs to prepare the fresh garden vegetables for a stir-fry. With Rosie and friends from South Africa, they washed great mounds of spinach, carrots, wild leeks, onions, and garlic. Then, armed with chopping boards, knives, and glasses of wine, they settled on the Feely Wine Lodge terrace in the sun. Soon chopping was interspersed with chatter and laughter and the vegetable mountains were effortlessly transformed into shreds.

'My beautiful granddaughters!' said Mum, seeing Sophia and Ellie come round the corner. She introduced them to the newcomers.

'It looks like the chopping is under control,' I said. 'Why don't we get the extra tables and set the table? *Allez les filles.*'

The sun was still bright on the vibrant lime-green vines of early summer. We brought extra tables and chairs from the tasting-room terrace and set an extended table on the Lodge deck. By the time we had finished, the shadows had grown, and the green had begun to fade with the lowering sun. The vineyard scene below us was like a great work of nature's art, an ever-changing vista through the hours and the seasons.

'This looks fantastic, Caro. Well done, girls,' said Sally as Sophia straightened up one of the settings.

It was simple but, with the weather and the scenery behind it, it was regal. Rosie placed a vase of wildflowers on the table.

'Perfect! Great teamwork!' I said, hearing footsteps on the terrace.

Sean had arrived in perfect time for aperitifs.

'Your garden is magnificent, Sean,' said Sally.

'I do what I can,' he replied modestly.

I refilled glasses for those already seated and offered Sean some wine. Rosie and Sally started stir-frying the vegetables.

Footsteps on the tasting-room terrace announced the arrival of the last guests. We did a round of introductions and I poured more wine.

'Cheers to our hosts!' said Gyles.

The clink of glasses rippled through the hiss of the stir-fry.

I passed the rice around the table then the stir-fry as it arrived fresh off the stovetop.

'Caro, is this the starter? Have you forgotten the meat?' asked Gyles.

We all laughed. He was winding me up. We ate a lot of vegetarian food. Organic meat was expensive, and we only ate organic, so meat was a special treat for us, not an everyday affair. With the organic rice, the mountain of stir-fried vegetables from the garden and a few bottles of our homegrown wine, we were well fed. Being together brought a deep sense of happiness. I missed not being able to have large family get-togethers like this more regularly. Our families were far flung across the globe.

After cheese and chocolate and fruit for dessert, the evening wound down. Guests staying off-site wandered back to their respective lodgings and Sean took Sophia and Ellie to bed.

Mum and I cleared the table while Sally and Rosie washed up. Being together made the task of cleaning up fun. We finished, said happy goodnights and I walked back across the courtyard with Mum.

'Thanks for sharing your lovely friends with us, Mum,' I said, giving her a hug.

'Thank you, Toots,' said Mum.

'The stir-fry worked well.'

'Well, Sean's garden is wonderful. The veggies taste so good fresh like that,' said Mum. 'But it is rather labour intensive, all that chopping.'

'But that was the best moment of the evening – you had such fun preparing the food together.'

'I suppose you're right – when everyone is together it *is* fun,' said Mum.

'It makes me think of a kitchen saying I saw recently: "More chopping, less shopping."'

'Ha ha, I like that,' said Mum.

'There's an English journalist and chef, Hugh Fearnley-Whittingstall. You know the guy who looks a bit like Sean?'

Mum nodded.

'He's famous for his fights to stop battery-reared chicken and to raise awareness of where seafood comes from and so on. In one of his TV series, he offered six people a transformation week to change their habits from instant packaged food to preparing it themselves. One of the women was retired but she still bought ready-made food from the supermarket even when she invited her friends around for dinner. At the end of the show, she said something like, "For ten years, I handed over the joy of cooking to the supermarkets. Now I remember how much fun it is, I feel like I've had ten years of enjoyment hijacked. I'll never buy ready-made again." She had tears rolling down her cheeks.'

'Oh, Toots! But you're so lucky to have Sean who cooks as well. I cook every night and it gets a bit tiring even though Dad washes the dishes.'

'I know. I agree. But I think it's because we aren't doing family food as a communal activity. If everyone is in the kitchen together it's fun. Plus, advertisers present food preparation as drudgery and serving up packaged food presented as your own as clever. But the hours spent driving to the supermarket and shopping to buy ready-made food totals more than it takes to create things from scratch in your own garden and kitchen, plus it's an ecological disaster. All that packaging, the carbon dioxide, the food miles...'

'Oh, darling,' said Mum, a little exasperated.

There was no doubt I could be obsessive. I found myself feeling guilty for throwing a few crumbs from the breadboard into the bin instead of into the compost. In John Seymour's book about his self-sufficient farm, *The Fat of the Land*, they washed their crockery in pure hot water so the used water could be given to the pigs. There were no chemical washing products and the pigs enjoyed the flavoured water. It was a total closed circuit with no waste. Pure self-sufficiency. I loved it. But we couldn't turn back the clock on our modern city-centric ways. City living did not allow for raising pigs on leftovers and washing water. We had to find new and better ways to keep challenging the status quo.

'Now I'm reflecting on this, perhaps we should do the dinner for the party ourselves. It would be convivial,' I said.

We had handed the main dinner for the Golden Wedding over to Luc and Martine Merlin at the Lion D'Or. All I was planning to do at home were the cheese course, dessert and coffee.

'Oh no, Toots! Absolutely not! You're too busy to even consider doing that. Look at you. You don't have a spare second to rub together. Anyway, we've confirmed with the Lion D'Or. No, darling!' said Mum with finality.

⤜⤛ ⤜⤛

The following evening corks popped on Feely sparkling wine as guests gathered on the terrace of the Lion D'Or. Sue and Ian Cameron, friends from Saussignac who had recently moved to Cunèges, a village nearby, joined us.

'We'll have to come and see you, Sue,' I said. 'I know it's only a short way away but it feels like another country. I preferred having you right here in Saussignac.'

'We would love to see you for tea or drinks,' said Sue in her beautiful English accent. 'You know it isn't very far. You could even walk to us.'

'Now that's the kind of challenge I like,' I said.

Sue and Ian were a wonderful, slightly eccentric couple. They had lived in India, Kenya, Zimbabwe, and Cyprus, doing many things, including coffee farming, then retired to France for a quieter life. Sue was a dynamo, a formidable force for good in our village, from the communal gardens to activities for the kids. Ian would walk their beloved

Labrador across the bottom of our farm most days in the early years, a familiar figure clad in corduroys, flat cap and walking stick, followed by his blond friend. We missed having them in our village.

I passed around the golden anniversary menu then ordered a whisky and soda for Dad and poured sparkling wine for Mum. As the guests perused the menu, I explained what it meant to those unfamiliar with French cuisine. Rosie held up her glass for more and Gyles proposed a toast to the happy couple, then a toast to absent friends and family. I saw tears in Mum and Dad's eyes and felt them in mine. We missed my sister and brother intensely in that moment.

Dad selected the *salade chèvre croustillant*, a roasted goat's cheese salad, and Mum the *nage d'escargots*, a snail and mushroom soup that was so good people talked about it for years. Both were paired with Feely *Générosité*, barrel-aged Semillon. For the main Dad chose *suprême de pintade*, a guinea-fowl dish with cream sauce, and Mum chose *magret au Xérès*, duck breast in sherry reduction sauce. Both mains were served with *pommes de terres Sarladaise et haricots verts*, potatoes fried in duck fat, a local tradition, and green beans. Feely *La Source* red wine was suggested with both. They chose different options each time. Perhaps being opposites was part of the secret of their partnership.

After an evening of banter and fine food, we walked home for speeches. Gyles cracked jokes and gave a short talk while we served the cheese course. Mum said a few words, then Dad spoke. He ended his heartfelt speech with a toast to Mum. After the toast he held up his glass and said, 'Don't leave me, Choekie' with tears in his eyes.

I felt a bolt of panic. Perhaps Dad knew something that we didn't know. Both of them were in good health but recently Mum had learned that one of her kidneys had shrivelled up and was no longer operational. With only one, she had to be careful with the anti-inflammatory tablets she took for her arthritis. She seemed more fragile than when I last saw them. I set that thought firmly aside and focused on serving the next course, *tarte aux abricots*, apricot tart, with Feely Saussignac dessert wine, a classic pairing that was always a hit.

'To Lyn and Cliff, fifty years of marriage. Here's to many more!' I said, holding up my dessert wine and wishing them one final toast, my eyes swimming with emotion. It was a great score. I read that more than half of French couples got divorced. Sean and I had come close to tearing apart a few times and we were only at fifteen.

After the party the days took on a timeless quality. We picnicked on the highest hill near Saussignac. We explored an unknown path to Cunèges to see if we could find Sue and Ian's new house. En route I hesitated at a stream that was flowing strong.

'Oh, come on, Caro,' said Sally, bending to take off her shoes and socks. Jeans folded to the knee, feet bare and walking shoes in hand, she waded in. 'It's delicious! Refreshing! Come on!'

After fording the stream, we crossed a forest and followed a farm road up into the village of Cunèges. I didn't know which house was Sue and Ian's, so we walked around the village looking for the finest garden. Thinking I had found it, I knocked on the door.

'*J'arrive,*' came a voice of fine English-accented French. Bingo.

'How lovely to see you! Come in, come in!' said Sue.

'Oh no, Sue, with our muddy shoes we won't come inside. We dropped by to see where you are,' I said.

'Well, come and see the garden at least,' said Sue, leading us around to the back gate. 'What about water for everyone?' she asked, already heading inside for it.

The garden was a perfect blend of French chic and English cottage garden, with benches strategically placed for views of rambling roses and scenic plantings. An organised *potager* bursting with vegetables nestled towards the back and an old barrel for collecting rainwater hugged the stone wall. Sue returned with a tray of glasses, and we slaked our thirst. They had transformed their house and garden in Saussignac, and they were doing the same here. Given that Sue was over seventy and Ian over eighty, it was even more awe-inspiring.

Halfway back to Saussignac, Mum said she wanted to be collected. It was unlike my mum to drop out – usually she was raring to go. I knew she was worried about Foo and Wade, but this seemed a bit more. I felt another bolt of fear.

That evening Mum owned up to a terrible toothache. She had been keeping it quiet to avoid worrying everyone, but it hadn't gone away. I called around for a dentist appointment. The best option I could find for an 'emergency' appointment was in a few weeks. They would be back in Canada by then. I knew dentist services in rural France were bad and now I realised just how bad. John and Morag, doctor friends from Canada, organised an antibiotic to control the infection and strong painkillers so Mum could tough it out until they got home. I felt awful that we could do nothing, but John assured me it would be

OK and perhaps better to have it dealt with by the dentist Mum knew. I was relieved that Mum's slowdown wasn't something more sinister.

While I had been with Mum, John, and Morag, talking about the options for Mum's tooth, Sean had come in from the vineyard and was catching up on his email on my computer.

He looked up with a frown.

'Did you know you have the fourth of July entered twice?'

'No,' I replied.

'Well, you'd better check it out.'

He got out of the chair, and I sat down to look at my booking sheet.

'Oh my God!' I said. 'I've booked a Médoc tour and Play Winemaker on the same day. What am I going to do?'

'You have to cancel one of them,' said Sean.

'But I can't – everything is booked. The Coopers are staying in Saussignac for two nights specially to do the winemaker day, and the Médoc day is all booked and has been for months – we'll never get appointments for another day at this stage in peak season,' I said. 'OMG. What am I going to do? Couldn't you do one of the days?'

'You know I can't. I don't have a day to spare this time of year and I wouldn't know where to start with giving a full-day tour. I can bail you out for a short visit, but I can't do it for a long one.'

My stomach clenched with stress.

'What the heck am I going to do?'

Sean lifted his eyebrows in a gesture that said, 'I don't know but you're on your own with this one.'

I couldn't push either a day forward or back as the days were packed with bookings.

The Médoc was the left bank of the Bordeaux area, the long finger that follows the Gironde estuary up to the sea. I was due to accompany the group in their car to do scene-setting en route but the visits would be with the *chateaux'* own guides. I reasoned that the clients could still do the day as planned and booked but without me. It was the only way out of the mess.

I steeled my stomach, picked up the phone and explained my mistake, then offered to come over with details of the visits, maps, and a guidebook to give the context to the visits that I would have done with them if I had been there on the day.

For the following hours I was consumed by my mistake.

'What's wrong, Toots?' asked my mum. 'You seem distracted.'

'Oh, Mum, I made a double booking. It's a bit of a disaster.'

'Oh, Toots, darling! I'm so sorry. You're so busy and all our guests have made things even more hectic for you.'

'No, Mum. It's a stupid mistake. I shouldn't have made it in the first place and in the second I should have picked it up ages ago.'

'Is there anything I can do?' asked Mum.

'I need to sort it out myself... Actually, since I'll be out this evening perhaps you could do dinner?' I said.

'Of course,' said Mum.

'Thanks, Mum. Sorry to rope you into work on your holiday, especially when you're not feeling so good.'

Mum had been setting tables, washing linen, emptying my dishwasher in the tasting room, sewing buttons, and helping in every direction. I had kept some days clear, but we also needed to keep the revenue coming in. We had created an organisation that needed constant feeding, loans, bottling costs, social charges, laboratory fees; a never-ending torrent that needed to be paid, and if we weren't working it wasn't.

'It's nothing. We're worried about you, Toots. You work so hard. There seems to be no end to your days. We see you working at six in the morning and eleven at night. We don't want you to get burnout.'

'He he,' I laughed nervously. 'It's better than being worried that we aren't getting the business. I know how hard it was to get the ball rolling in the first place.'

That evening I took a gift bottle of Feely *methode traditionelle* sparkling wine and a profusion of apologies and explained the itinerary in detail. I offered my pocket guides that went with the day and refunded them in full. The clients tried to be understanding but their disappointment was obvious.

I needed to get a grip. I went through all my reservations with a fine toothcomb to be sure that I hadn't repeated the error. I hadn't, but it didn't console me much. Managing the comings and goings in the accommodation, visits on the farm and beyond, and holding down the administration and marketing of our wine business, at the same time as trying to be a wife, mother, and daughter, had me swamped.

Mum and Dad and their friends left, and the season spun into high gear. My nightmares about dying returned and if a nightmare didn't wake me then a feverish hot sweat did. With the lack of sleep, I felt like I couldn't cope, and my temper flared at almost nothing. I put it down to the stress of the growing business and resolved to have an apprentice in place before the start of the following season.

CHAPTER 7

Mothering and Memory

With high summer I took cold showers. They left me feeling awake and alive. My sister Foo sent intermittent updates about the progress of her husband Wade. A court case was brewing but it looked like it would take years. Foo posted bail and Wade was able to live a 'normal' life, but the case was looming like a sword over his head. Weeks turned into months. As summer drew to a close and autumn took hold, I felt grateful getting into a hot shower. It was a gift of energy that something and someone had to generate. Like a car and a phone, it was a luxury, not a right.

I found a natural sleeping remedy at my local pharmacy. It helped, but I was still depressed, tired, and irritable.

'I don't know what is wrong with me,' I said to Sean. 'I've been so ratty lately. I'm not sleeping well.'

He looked at me knowingly, as if to say, 'You think we hadn't noticed?'

'Maybe it's menopause,' he said. 'You should look it up on the internet.'

I did a search and found that the symptoms I had been feeling for almost a year were signs that I was in 'perimenopause', the phase before menopause that could last years. Perimenopause created physical and emotional imbalance due to hormonal changes. The joyful list included hot flushes, irritability, depression, disturbed sleep, loss of libido, incontinence, weight gain, tension, anxiety, hair loss, memory lapses, irregular heartbeat, thoughts of suicide, dreams of dying and more. Longer-term problems from it included osteoporosis. Almost all the glorious signs had manifested in me.

Since the start of menstruation I had wished it would end; now I wished it wouldn't. Thirty years before, when it started, I thought I was dying. It was a time when we didn't talk about things like sex and menstruation. The day my period struck I was out with my dad. No matter how serious I thought it was, I would never have talked to my dad about bleeding on my underwear. I stuffed toilet paper into my undies and prayed that I wouldn't die. When I got home – fortunately still alive – I told my mum about the bleeding, and she delved into the medicine cupboard. Sanitary pads coming from the place she went when we were sick, confirmed my hunch that it was a bad omen for my health. Before she could explain anything, my mum was called away. Foo was home from boarding school for the weekend and explained what it was, along with her girls-only-boarding-school version of the birds and the bees.

With this new phase I felt like I had when menstruation started – unprepared and uninformed. Why had no one told me about it? My menopause journey was relatively early on the bell curve of womankind, like my menstruation had been. My sister hadn't been through menopause yet, even though she was older than me; neither had most of my friends. I had heard about hot flushes – usually spoken of with a nervous laugh – but I hadn't heard about the monster that had taken hold of me.

Perimenopause had me so depressed and stressed I considered all manner of ways of getting away from the infernal pressure, even thinking I would be better off in jail away from the stress of my life, or in one of our vats filled with carbon dioxide, in the peace of that long goodnight.

Now I knew there was a reason for my strange behaviour that went beyond stress. With that knowledge I could do things to help myself cope. Top of the list were exercise, eating healthily, and limiting alcohol intake. With the manic schedule required by our growing business, I had let my running routine fall by the wayside. I was walking to school with my daughters but that wasn't enough. I needed to exercise more. Many websites suggested yoga and a friend offered to take me to her yoga class. I tried it and enjoyed it, but it was too far and too time-consuming. I couldn't afford to take a whole morning out of my schedule. The yoga idea slipped away but we ate healthily, and I stopped drinking coffee. I laughed at a quote sent by a friend, 'It doesn't matter if the glass is half full or half empty – there is always room for more wine', but I cut back all the same; the hot flushes were worse after a couple of glasses.

While I toughed it out with perimenopause, Sean was finding Zen in our second vegetable garden. Our first had failed despite great effort. It was a patterned geometric wonder 'worthy of Versailles' according to Sonia, our neighbour. Mental labour – mathematical triangulations for perfect proportions – preceded physical labour. We dug, added horse manure from a neighbour, then dug again. Our vegetables were a disaster. Thinking like Dubliners, we had set the garden in the sunniest spot of the farm. On the high Garrigue in South-West France, the sunniest spot was perfect for scrubby herbs: thyme, rosemary, lavender, and sage; our rosemary bushes became so large and thick they were more like trees than shrubs. But it was too hot and dry for vegetables, especially softies like lettuce. They didn't have a hope.

Sean moved the garden down to a half-shaded field relatively close to the house. It was full of thistles and didn't look good, but the middle shade it offered, and the proximity, made it a sensible choice. He began with a modest bed and grew a few veg. The following year he increased his garden and his yield. The following year he did it again. One foot at a time, the garden expanded into a glorious profusion. He was like the lead character in Jean Giono's 'The Man who Planted Trees'.

When we started our adventure, it was a high-five achievement when we had a dinner produced exclusively from our farm. Now there were times in the year when everything came from our garden, and I felt slighted if I had to buy vegetables. There was something deeply satisfying about harvesting from the backyard.

Sean grew 50 kilograms of potatoes - almost enough for our year's supply, countless pumpkins, butternuts, beetroot, onions, garlic, chickpeas and the usual suspects of tomatoes, courgettes, lettuce, and beans. He became possessive about his garden.

'Don't touch anything. Tell me what you want, and I'll get it,' he said.

I was the idiot that would pull up lettuces that weren't fully ready or harvest tomatoes before they had reached their heavenly peak.

'As of today, you can pick all the baby tomatoes you want,' he said. 'They're almost over. We need to eat them or preserve them.'

Ellie and I obeyed, pulling luscious baby tomatoes from the bushes and eating as we went.

'One for the basket, one for me,' I said, popping another into my mouth.

'It's like a big market where everything is free,' said Ellie.

'Except if you count Papa's work. He enjoys it so it's not really "work", but it does take muscles, brains, and time. But you're right – it's free in the sense that we don't have to pay money for it. Also, it's right here, and when we pick it and eat it straight away, the vitamins are higher, and it tastes better.'

'And they store better out here than inside. We've been eating tomatoes since early summer and now it's autumn,' added Ellie.

'Good point,' I said. 'Usually, they keep better on the plant than off but if we leave them too long, they'll still rot.'

'And,' said Ellie, giving me a professorial look over her glasses, 'there's no transport, no carbon dioxide to bring them to us.'

'Good thinking, Ellie,' I responded, surprised that she had thought of this aspect.

'You know we're doing the law project at school, trying to work out ways to decrease carbon dioxide emissions?'

I nodded, realising her school project must have helped to spark this reflection. With the United Nations Climate Change Conference Talks in Paris looming, the subject of how to decrease carbon dioxide emissions was getting more airtime.

'We might even go to Paris if they choose our project. Then we'll visit parliament, and we'll get to have the *goûter* at parliament.'

'I wonder if they have their own garden there,' I said.

'If we go, I'll ask,' said Ellie.

'That would be great. Sorry, Ellie, I have to go,' I said, feeling sad to leave. I was enjoying our chat, but I had a large group arriving in a few minutes.

I finished washing the tomatoes as the minivan of guests arrived. After another packed day, my nerves were jangling. I worried that my stress was visible, but the feedback forms were glowing. The only suggestion for improvement was to iron the tablecloths. Usually, I could rely on drip-dry to leave them wrinkle-free but rain the day before had meant I had to use the drier.

When I came in that evening, Sean was in the kitchen chopping a mountain of fresh spinach from the garden. He didn't greet me or kiss me as we would have when I got home when we lived in the city. We were like passing ships in the night. I was lucky if he grunted at me in the morning when I took a cup of tea up for him. There was barely a connection.

'You need to take care of your daughters,' Sean said. 'Teach them how to look after their hair. Ellie's hair is in a knot again.' He didn't even look up.

Ellie came through. The entire middle section of her hair, from neck level to lower shoulder blades, was a solid mat of dreadlocks.

'I recommend cutting the hair,' I said.

'But they love long hair,' replied Sean.

'You love their long hair,' I said.

Sean loved the girls' long hair, but I didn't want it. Long hair was a responsibility. It needed to be brushed morning and night and washed regularly. In winter they needed to blow-dry it and neither of them did. If I didn't dry it for them, they went to bed with wet heads. But they were attached to it, perhaps from years of positive reinforcement by Sean. Sophia had less hair and was more responsible. Ellie needed supervision – if I didn't remind her, she didn't brush her hair, and even with reminding she sometimes didn't do it; she could be a rebel. A few weeks before, I had spent an hour, and half a bottle of conditioner, teasing out a knotted section. I really didn't want to go through that again. A wave of anger surged through me.

'If you like the long hair so much, you get the knots out,' I shouted at Sean.

I did not have time for long hair. Violence rose inside me; frustration that I wasn't being the mother I should be thrashed up against the pressure I felt about getting ready for a group arriving in The Wine Lodge that evening and another group for a tour the following day. I still hadn't got to the emails that had come in. I hadn't had time to respond to the previous day's emails despite getting up at six and not stopping. Clients expected responses in 24 hours. I tried to do that and if the pressure was too much, like now, within 48 at worst. I slammed the door and went to find Ellie, who had disappeared back up the stairs.

She and I closed ourselves into the shower room and I poured the other half of the bottle of conditioner on to the knot and began teasing the hair out section by section. I was as gentle as possible, but Ellie started crying, partly because of the tugging and partly because she was upset about the knot and my anger.

'We're going to have to cut it out,' I said. 'This is way worse than last time. You have to brush your hair morning and night. You have to be responsible, Ellie. You can't have long hair if you aren't going to look after it.'

I felt furious –with Sean, with a world that said they needed long hair, with Ellie, but most of all with myself.

We braved it out for an hour. Eventually Ellie was freezing, and I felt like I had arthritis I had been bent over her in the shower for so long. The knot was almost as big as it had been at the start, and we were both crying.

'I'm going to get the scissors. It's the only solution. The knot is too big,' I said.

Ellie cried even harder.

'It will grow back, Ellie, *ma chérie*,' I said.

'OK,' she said finally through her tears.

I wrapped her in a towel and went to fetch the shears.

I cut off the clump and tried to tidy it up around the edges then we sat on the bed exhausted. I hugged her small, towelled figure in a deep embrace and we stayed there, meditating, trying to find peace between us.

'I am so sorry, Ellie bug,' I said and held her closer.

Once we got a grip on ourselves, I dried what was left of her hair.

'It's not so bad,' she said, looking at herself in the mirror.

'No, you can barely see it,' I said. 'It will grow out in no time.'

I gave her another tight hug.

'Neither of us wants this to happen again so you have to brush it morning and night. I can't go through this again. Not ever.'

She nodded.

I hugged her again and we descended the stairs for our spinach dinner.

⁕⁂⁕

Along with the visits at our farm, the accommodation and organic wine, we offered multi-day tours and vineyard walking tours that went beyond our estate. I had recently found a new route for a walking tour around the area of Monbazillac that included a stop at Michelin-starred restaurant La Tour des Vents for lunch, a visit to an organic winery and a walk around the grounds of Monbazillac Castle.

I had done it a few times and it was becoming a favourite, but as I took off from the village of Monbazillac with my latest group we passed a farmer spraying herbicide on his vineyard and I wondered if it was such a good route after all. I led the group as far away as possible, but we could still smell the weedkiller. I felt anger boiling inside me. It was wrong that this farmer could legally pollute the air we were breathing with a carcinogen. In time we will not believe that humankind could have been so stupid. In *Harvest for*

Hope: A Guide to Mindful Eating, Jane Goodall wrote about how future generations would look back on this dark era of agriculture and ask in disbelief, 'How could we have ever believed that it was a good idea to grow our food with poisons?'

Our route took us through light woods and vineyards. As we walked, I explained the different plants and trees, especially those we used in biodynamics, like the nettle, willow, and horsetail.

'There's a hazel,' I said, pointing to a coppiced tree in the hedgerow of the adjacent pasture.

'Sometimes it's hard to tell it from other trees with similar shaped leaves until you get up close and see it has slightly furry leaves,' said Royce, a tall North American.

'Interesting,' I said. 'I never stopped to feel the leaves. Giving leaves textural consideration makes a lot of sense – it's another identification point.'

Another machine was lashing spray on to a vineyard up ahead. I considered an alternative route that was longer, but one of the group had owned up to a sore knee a few minutes before, so I was hesitant. As we got closer to the sprayer, I recognised the winegrower.

'Phew! We can pass,' I said. 'That is Kilian of Château Kalian, an organic vineyard. We'll have a bottle of his organic wine with lunch.'

We kept walking for a while then I called a break. I laid out my waterproof jacket and sat down to serve home-made elderflower cordial and organic biscuits.

The group's happy chatter filled the air while I located myself on the map before closing it into my backpack.

We set off again, picking up the pace, and came to a familiar fork in the road. Despite having done the walk many times, I experienced a momentary doubt about which way to go. I knew the route so well. I took the right fork but a few minutes later didn't recognise where we were. The person with the sore knee didn't need to walk any extra miles. I stopped and took the map out of my bag and tried to orientate myself. I couldn't work out where we were or where we needed to go. My brain shut down. I felt panic rising. We walked back to the fork so I could look at the signs.

'I'll look us up on my phone,' said Royce.

'Thanks, Royce,' I said.

'How many times did you say you've done this route, Caro?' asked Joyce, the lady with the sore knee.

'So many. I think I got disorientated because the seasons have changed since I was here last,' I said, my face going red with embarrassment.

Royce's phone showed to go back the way we had come. But it also showed we had such a long way to go to the restaurant and I knew that wasn't right. I hesitated. Had I got us that lost? Were we so far off our target? I doubted myself. For a few minutes I looked at my paper map and at the phone. Part of me said, 'Trust the new technology – it has to be right', and the other part said, 'Stick with your gut instinct'. I had to make a call.

'The way I originally took us is correct. The seasonal changes and new paintwork on the house disorientated me,' I said, sounding more convinced than I felt.

Joyce looked dubious. I didn't blame her. I led us back up the road, my heart racing. This had never happened to me, even on a brand-new route. I was always sure of my direction and this one was a regular, familiar route for me. As we popped out of a forest, I saw the restaurant in the distance and light-headed relief swept through me. The map on the phone had the restaurant address as a place completely different to the actual location of the restaurant.

I chalked another negative mark down to the awful transformation I was going through; perimenopause symptoms included memory lapses. Or perhaps it was nervous-system disruption from the chemicals being sprayed next to our path at the start of the walk. I would never know. I wondered how I would regain the confidence and satisfaction of my group, although being on the right path helped.

At La Tour des Vents, nibbles of potato and *aioli* - a garlic mayonnaise - and tiny wraps of smoked trout, preceded an amuse-bouche of *mousse de courgette et fausse terre Parmesan* -dark savoury Parmesan biscuit crushed to look like soil, and crumbled over courgette mousse. Then we delighted in a starter of tomato soup laced with olives and *jambon de Bayonne*, perfectly paired with a white wine from Brigitte Soulier of Château La Robertie, a feisty woman I had got to know through a Women in Wine group. We continued the feast with guinea-fowl fillet wrapped around a langoustine with a flamed whisky langoustine sauce, stuffed courgette flower and spinach with cream, paired with red wine from Château Kalian, the winegrower we had seen en route. With fine wine flowing, my memory lapse faded like the wisps of mist on the river below us. By the end my guests seemed to have forgotten, but I had not.

At home I checked in with one of our hazels. The leaves had always looked flat but close up they were furry. I rubbed a leaf between my fingers. It smelt like hazelnut.

Now I went around feeling and sniffing the leaves of other plants and took more notice of the texture.

My experience with Ellie's hair had shown I wasn't keeping it together on the family front, and the walk, and my double booking, showed I wasn't on the work front either, but I couldn't let the lapses destroy my confidence. I had a packed schedule through to the end of October and harvest was in full swing. We had harvested the Sauvignon Blanc and the Semillon. The reds would be next. I wondered how I would make it through the next four weeks. I had never relished winter; now I found myself looking forward to it. I picked a lavender flower from the pot outside my tasting-room door and drew the calming aroma into my being.

CHAPTER 8

Take Ten Deep Breaths

A petite woman with jet-black hair and a tall, slim man with sandy-brown hair walked up the Gardonne platform with suitcases.

'You must be Caro. I'm Chris and this is Dave,' said the woman in a warm voice, introducing them both with a flourish. We shook hands.

'Welcome to Aquitaine,' I said. 'It's great to meet you.'

We chatted as we made our way to Château Feely. 'We have limited time to travel since Dave still works full-time. I don't think he will ever stop working,' Chris said and gave a delicious laugh that filled the car.

Her laughter set me at ease. Their good humour was what I needed for the week ahead.

'I'll run through the itinerary, so you know what is happening over the next few days,' I said. 'Tomorrow is the

Wine Adventure at Château Feely, so you'll spend the day learning about wine at our organic vineyard. Wednesday you go to Bergerac for the market and the cookery class with Stéphane at Table du Marché. Thursday we'll be harvesting our Merlot for Résonance. There'll be noise in the courtyard from around five in the morning and lots to see. Then we go to St-Émilion for the *grand cru classés* tour. Friday's a rest day for you. Phew. Perhaps you can take a relaxing walk to the Lion D'Or for lunch. Saturday's our vine-shareholder harvest day with a picnic for lunch then the harvest dinner in Saussignac. Sunday is a vineyard walking tour with lunch. That takes us to Monday, when I'll bring you back to the station where you just arrived. How does that sound?'

'Perfect for us,' said Chris. 'But it sounds like quite a packed agenda for you, Caro.'

'No worries. I'm used to it,' I said, feeling a little increase in my pulse all the same.

The next day there were six other people booked on the Wine Adventure. We gathered on the terrace of the tasting room for introductions.

'I can tell the difference between white and red,' said one person, and the deck reverberated with laughter.

'I practise wine-tasting every night,' said Jeff, another guest, setting off another round of laughter.

When sparks of humour flashed during the introductions, I knew it was going to be a good day; that there was an energy and dynamic in the group. We set off for our walk around the vines. Half-way up a row I stopped and picked up two flints, rubbed them together and passed them to the nearest person.

'Rub them together then sniff the stone. You'll pick up a flinty character, like the smell after a gun has gone off; for some people it reminds them of the smell of crackers or fireworks. That flinty aroma is a classic giveaway of Chablis, Chardonnay grown on flinty soil in north-west Burgundy. Now when you smell that on a wine, you will know it grew in soil that had flint stone in it.'

'That's amazing. I smelt that aroma on a Chablis last week,' said Jeff.

'You'll smell it on our *Silex* and *Générosité*, two Semillon wines you'll taste later,' I said. 'But the taste of *terroir* does not show up so clearly in all wine. The wine must be farmed naturally. Any ideas why?'

They shook their heads.

'At the rock level there are critters that break down rocks and turn them into soluble minerals for the plants to feed on. This soil life contributes to the taste of *terroir* but also to the nutrition. Recently I read that a basket of fruit and vegetables today has the same calories but around half the essential vitamins and minerals of the same basket in the 1950s.' Eyes widened. 'Modern intensive chemical farming impoverishes the land. Done for long enough it will turn a farm into a desert.'

'But isn't farming naturally more labour intensive?' asked Dave.

'Yes. Hand-weeding this acre of Cabernet Sauvignon takes around three man-days and needs to be done two or three times a season. For older vines we use a mechanical hoe on the tractor but for baby organic vines the only solution is by hand. We think it's worth it. I can say that since Sean does most of the back-breaking weeding.' I paused for the laughter to pass then continued.

'The phase of "growing up", the first fifteen years of the vine's life, is important to farm organically for long-term health and capacity to resist disease. The vine's life cycle follows similar phases to a person's life cycle, and this is the phase of building its body. By not using herbicide we offer them the opportunity to grow up healthy plus it encourages the roots to go deeper.'

'Why is that Caro?' asked Chris.

'Hoeing cuts the weeds out but also cuts the surface roots of the vines and encourages them to plunge deeper. Herbicide does the opposite, it kills the plants on the surface, leaving the space open for the vine roots so they're not encouraged to go deep. The main weedkiller used, glyphosate, was classed as a "probable" carcinogen by the World Health Organization recently.'

'I read about that. It's crazy that it can still be used,' said Chris. Some of the others in the group looked surprised.

'Fascinating. I never thought about any of this,' said Jeff.

'Chemical fertiliser sprinkled on the surface also encourages shallow roots,' I continued, on a roll with my audience's attention. 'The roots stay where the easy food is. Like us when we're attracted to high-fat, high-salt, fast food, the vine is taken in by this fake food that will make it unhealthy. Chemical fertiliser turns the vine's life upside down. The vine is naturally orientated to the sky. It wants to reach for the sun and the stars, forging upwards by all means possible. By pouring man-made fertiliser – the famous mix of NPK: nitrogen, potassium, and phosphate – at its feet, we make it focus on the ground instead. The vine can make ninety-four percent of its dry matter from what it gets from the sky. It can take gases from the air, energy from the sun. Giving it fast food on the ground is like saying to someone, "Sit on the couch and we'll provide fast food and salty snacks on tap."'

'What a great analogy', said Jeff laughing.

'Yes, and just like us when we eat salty food, the mineral salt in the chemical fertiliser makes the vine thirsty. It takes up more water and holds more water in its cells – like we do when we have too much salt. It's not good for us and it's really not good for the vine since excess water makes it get fungal disease. Fungal disease can destroy our crop and even kill the vine. That makes conventional chemical farmers turn to systemic fungicides which can be nervous system disruptors.' I paused. 'Wow, I've been off on a tangent. You can tell I have a lot to say about why you should choose organic.'

'Thanks Caro. I'm learning so much,' said Chris.

'What about beneficial fungi in the soil? I was reading about wild orchids on your website?' asked another guest.

'You are spot on. Fungicides also kill the mycorrhizae, a magical relationship between fungi and plant-root systems that helps them access nutrients in the soil. The mycorrhizae stock and distribute water and nutrients to the plants in exchange for carbohydrates - sucrose and glucose from photosynthesis - and they act as a communication network between plants. Research has shown that mycorrhizal networks transport carbon, phosphorus, nitrogen, water, and defence compounds -compounds that combat attack - from plant to plant. They're especially beneficial for plants in nutrient-poor soils and the best wine grapes are grown on relatively poor soil. Orchids need mycorrhizae. Wild orchids started to return to Chateau Feely after three years of organic farming. They were an indicator that our soil health was returning.'

'Amazing,' said Chris. 'You and Sean must have been so happy to see them.'

'We were. They are beautiful too. Anyway, to finish off what started this tangent, a third thing that can keep the vine's roots on the surface is drip irrigation. The French AOC or Appellation d'Origine Contrôlée, what we call PDO or Protected Designation of Origin in English, includes a law of no irrigation, which means that doesn't happen much here.'

'Why no irrigation?' asked Dave.

'Back in 1936, when France set up the appellations based on the traditional wine areas, including names you know like Burgundy, Bordeaux, Bergerac, they wanted AOC to be something that reflected the *terroir*, the place the wine came from and the unique vintage conditions. Today many of us natural winegrowers are leaving the AOC because we find it incoherent to say no irrigation for *terroir* and at the same time allow chemical fertilisers, herbicides, and systemic pesticides.'

'I have to agree with you natural winegrowers. What a crazy contrast. "You can't use water but you can use carcinogens",' said Jeff.

I raised my eyebrows and nodded.

'Any other questions before we move on?' I asked.

'Caro, can you explain what that word you used, *terroir*, means?' said Chris.

'Sure. *Terroir* is the combination of soil, microclimate, plant, and the human hand that give a unique flavour. These four elements are interrelated and can also influence each another. Take the soil of this Cabernet vineyard: it has an unusual mix of clay, limestone, flint stone and gravel. The hot sun on the flint stone and gravel creates more heat and those stones keep the heat for longer overnight than a vineyard of clay or one of clay and limestone. That flint and gravel are part of the heat secret of this zone – the stones influence the microclimate. This is the best plot on the farm for Cabernet Sauvignon because of that, but also because it's a plateau so it gets good sun all day. In addition, because of its shape and inclination – almost flat – we were able to go north–south with our rows for best sun exposure. That gives us full morning sun on the east side and afternoon sun on the west side.' I held my hands either side of the vine row to show what I meant.

As I turned to move us on to the next vineyard, I noticed a wild salad and stopped to point it out. 'That red-stemmed plant is wild purslane. It's beautiful to look at but also good to eat. It has great crunch and tang, a fantastic addition to any salad. Go ahead and taste if you like,' I said, snapping off a piece and popping it into my mouth.

Chris did the same and crunched it. 'Very tasty,' she said.

'It's great that you can pick wild salads under your vines. I guess that's only possible because you farm organic?' asked another member of the group.

'You guessed right,' I said.

As we walked, I spotted a few missed bunches of white so the visitors could taste the characteristics of the different grapes we grew: Sauvignon Blanc with its zesty grapefruit character; Semillon with its stone-fruit sweetness; then the ones still waiting to be picked, the Merlot heady with blackberry and plum, and the Cabernet Sauvignon redolent of cassis.

I ended the outside part of the tour with talking about the different farming methods. For me it was the most important part of what we did. Organic was not merely about stopping the pesticides and their terrible repercussions of cancer, nervous-system disruption and endocrine – reproductive – disruption; it was about better nutrition, about rebuilding our soil, about leaving a healthy planet for the next generation.

A short tasting course, the wine and food lunch, and an afternoon on winemaking followed. The tours had evolved over the years with our increasing knowledge and increasing range. We had our first no-sulphites-added wine, *Grâce*, which offered the opportunity to talk about natural wine and why 'no sulphites added' could be interesting for a wine lover.

'Thank you so much, Caro. That was a great day!' said Chris when we finished late afternoon.

'It's a pleasure Chris. Tomorrow you and Dave are in Bergerac for the cookery school. Thursday we'll be in Saint Emilion. Friday you have your free day and I'll be preparing for our harvest weekend. We're expecting around 60 people. It's going to be fun.'

As I described it all I realised how much I had taken on that week. I usually liked a packed schedule. Now I wasn't so sure. The effects of perimenopause, my memory lapse, and my bad temper with my family, had sapped my energy.

As if reading my mind, Chris replied, 'I hope you don't mind me saying this but with everything you have going on, you need to relax to be able to cope. You should try taking ten deep breaths. Breathing deeply has a calming effect.'

'Thanks, Chris. I'll try it,' I said, barely taking a breath before racing on to the next thing. 'So tomorrow I'll see you for breakfast at eight, then I'll take you down to the station at nine so you can head into Bergerac.'

'Perfect,' said Chris.

I could see her thinking, 'Like hell she's going to try that deep breathing. Did she even hear what I said?'

But as soon as she and Dave left me alone in the tasting room, I tried her trick. After ten deep breaths I felt more relaxed. With my body and spirit calmed, I started the clean-up.

***

Sean was making good progress with our white fermentations. The Sauvignon Blanc was looking like it could be the best we had ever made, but yields were low. We had estimated our wine production for the year, and it was not good, particularly on the Merlot. The cold, wet spring had hit us badly. The flowers did not fertilise properly, so the fruit set was meagre. Ironically bad fruit set can be good for quality as the grapes that are left get more attention from the vine and have better aeration. I consoled myself that our wine was about quality.

We had decided that hand-picking everything was a priority for the following year. I contacted our CUMA agricultural co-op president to negotiate to stop our machine-picking contract. If everything went well, Thursday would be the last time we would have a harvest machine in our courtyard. We could not wait to say *au revoir*.

Thursday dawned dry but overcast. The starry dome that usually provided the backdrop for our morning harvest dance was missing. Sean and I moved through the steps mechanically and the harvest machine did the same. We finished in good time, well before I needed to leave for St-Émilion. I had provided Chris and Dave with breakfast supplies the night before so they could serve themselves. Despite the morning going smoothly I had so much in my head, so many different things juggling for my attention – what I had to do that day, things required for the harvest weekend – that I felt uneasy.

With the grapes safe in the winery, Chris, Dave, and I waved goodbye to Sean, and set off for St-Émilion. I parked the car between two low-level marker rocks on the free parking near the Porte Brunet and we walked into town through the medieval city gate. I loved coming into St-Émilion this way; the promise of a gateway to somewhere was exciting. In spite of having offered guided visits there for years, I still found new alleyways with stunning views, unexpected dry-stone walls studded with wildflowers, or medieval doors, when I had spare time to wander.

We ambled to the central square, stopping at different points to appreciate the vistas and so that I could point out key landmarks.

'Château Ausone, a top estate in St-Émilion, is the grey roof you see at the edge of town. It was started by Ausonius in around 350. The bell tower you see is the monolithic church carved from the solid rock by Émilion, hermit monk and namesake of St-Émilion, who settled here in 750. The square tower to the left is the King's Tower, built in 1200 for an English king, John, one of Eleanor of Aquitaine's sons. The English rule, from 1152 to 1453, started when Eleanor, the heiress of our region, married a toy boy, Henry, who become King of England soon after. Have you heard about her?'

'A little. She has quite a racy history,' replied Chris.

'Indeed. She was married to Louis VII, King of France, in Bordeaux city when she was fifteen years old. Fourteen years later she convinced the Pope to annul the marriage on the count of consanguinity and she married Henry. She outlived eight of her ten children.'

We took a commune path through the vineyards to our first winery visit. The winegrower led us out into his vines where I spotted a wild spinach plant and pointed it out. Chris bent to pick a leaf so she could try it, like we had tasted some of the wild salads between our vines two days before, and the winegrower dived like Superman to stop her putting it into her mouth.

'I would prefer you didn't eat it. We sprayed the vineyard yesterday to stop fungal disease,' he said.

Chris dropped the leaf like it was a snake about to strike. After all I had said about pesticides, she knew this was not something to be messed with.

Spraying had to stop at least three weeks before harvest. The fruit was safe from fungal disease once it did the *veraison* – changing colour from green to purple for red grapes and from green to yellow for white grapes – but some winegrowers, like this one, sprayed a systemic fungicide immediately after harvest so they could keep their foliage healthy for as long as possible, theoretically to allow the vines time to take back the nutrients before the winter sleep. Ironically that would mean that the natural breakdown of the leaves, and hence the health of their soil, would be damaged since fungus forms a key part of the natural composting cycle.

Later, over lunch on the main square, we chatted about our first visit, about harvest that morning, and about life. After a couple of days together, Dave and Chris were becoming friends. I checked the time on my phone and realised we had been chatting so much we were running late for our next visit. I paid the bill, and we raced back up to the car. As I took off, the car hit something then lurched forward and wobbled down the road.

'That's the tyre gone,' said Dave.

'Heck,' I said, holding back the expletive that I wanted to use and pulling over on to the grass verge. 'A burst tyre is one of my tour nightmares. Thank goodness I'm with wonderful people like you!'

In my haste I had forgotten about the marker rock. In my nightmare I was with difficult clients, and we were under pressure to get to the airport for their flight home. I stood on the side of the road thinking, *What will I do? How do I even change a tyre?* I had no idea. Then I woke up in a cold sweat. Now here we were with a real puncture, and we would be even later for our visit but at least I was with friends.

'Ten deep breaths, Caro,' said Chris.

We all laughed.

'Dave, do you know anything about changing tyres?' I asked.

'A little,' said Dave. 'I'll give it a go.'

'Thank you! I'll call Antoine and let him know we'll be late.'

Antoine Mariau was the winemaker at Château Cadet-Bon, where we were due. He picked up.

'Antoine, I have burst my tyre.'

'I will come over and help you,' he said without hesitation. 'Where are you?'

I explained, and in minutes Antoine's small white van turned up the road snug between St-Émilion's ramparts and vineyards. He was a dark, handsome twenty-something. We got on well. With my regular visits to his vineyard, he had become a friend. I introduced him to Chris and Dave.

He and Dave reviewed the 'biscuit' replacement tyre Dave had found in the boot of my car and the car jack. They were installing the jack when a man in shorts and flip-flops sauntered past.

'I'll do it for you. I'm a mechanic from Poland,' he said. 'I can do this in my sleep.'

Dave and Antoine handed the task over with relief and we formed an observation committee on the sidelines.

'He knows what he's doing,' said Antoine.

'He sure does,' said Dave.

'You don't need me. I'll head back and see you at the vineyard in a few minutes,' said Antoine.

'Thank you so much, Antoine,' I said.

'It's my pleasure. But, in fact, I did nothing,' he said, laughing. He jumped into his van and sped off.

The Polish mechanic swiftly finished the job.

'You saved the day. I can't thank you enough,' I said, giving him a token of appreciation. I felt like hugging him.

'Oh, it was nothing. Like I said, I can do this in my sleep,' he said.

Dave and I carefully checked for marker stones, and I cautiously took off again.

'And so, I find that my wine tour nightmare turns out to be a great opportunity to meet people and chat with friends on the roadside in St-Émilion,' I said.

Dave and Chris laughed. I was injecting humour into the situation, but I was rattled – I didn't usually forget things like marker stones on the road in front of where I had parked.

At Château Cadet-Bon, Antoine led us into the barrel *chai*, a semi-underground cellar carved into the limestone with a wood-panelled roof shaped in a sensuous curve. The ancient stone and modern, organic roundness finished in natural material were a perfect blend of old and new *and* it was filled with fabulous wine in beautiful French oak barrels.

Antoine explained how he made the wine, the ageing and his barrel selection process – a fine art. For each vineyard and each grape type he had preferred oak forests and preferred barrel makers based on years of careful selection.

Since our first year with a badly behaved Merlot tank that had me breaking out in eczema and insomnia, I knew that ageing in oak could truly change a wine. It helped soften the tannin through micro-oxygenation and made the wine weightier and creamier so it could match slightly heavier food. Aromas of barrel ageing can include vanilla, chocolate, toast, sweet spices, and even coconut, depending on the origin of the wood, how it was dried, and how much 'toasting' - the burning of the inside of the barrel - the wood has had.

As winegrowers we were aware that one kind of oak was different to another, but with the price of six new barrels equivalent to an entry level car, Sean and I were not experts in the field. Here at Cadet-Bon, on the other hand, it was a high art. With his consultant, Antoine assessed the barrels they purchased each year, comparing barrel maker, toasting and forest with overall quality, taste, and effect on the wine. With at least 30 new barrels each year, they had the luxury of comparison.

'Well, enough talk about barrels. What about some tasting?' said Antoine as he dipped his glass pipette, called a 'wine thief', into a honey-coloured barrel. It slowly filled with deep purple wine then he closed it by placing his thumb over the hole at the top, lifted it and released a sample into my glass before stopping the flow with a deft thumb and doing the same for Chris and Dave.

My nose descended into the glass; the aroma was deep and mineral with liveliness of fresh fruit and rich spiciness of plum pudding. When I tasted, there was a marked difference to their usual Merlot on limestone: the tannins formed two parallel lines on my tongue and were spicier and more astringent than usual. I lifted my eyebrows then moved towards the spittoon at the end of the row of barrels.

'Delicious,' said Chris.

'Jupille forest,' said Antoine. He closed the bung and moved to another barrel.

'This barrel is the same wine, the same barrel maker, the same toasting as the other limestone Merlot, but the oak is from the Tronçais forest,' said Antoine, moving to the next barrel and doing the same again.

'Incredible,' I said after sniffing and tasting the sample. 'The tannin is completely different. It's more integrated and less sappy.'

'I am blown away,' said Dave. 'I would never have thought the forest the barrel came from could make such a difference.'

'Yes, on the whole I prefer,' said Antoine, skipping the 'it' in the French way like he sometimes did. 'But I like to have a little Jupille. It adds to the blend.'

The Tronçais forest was close to Jupille – they were both in the central part of France. We could taste their *terroir* talking.

'It takes all the different parts, the different barrels, grapes, and soils, to make the final blend. Two Merlots planted just a few hundred metres apart can be totally different. The Merlot on limestone gives us a wine that is long and taut, filled with freshness and vivacity, while the Merlot on the deeper clay is round, full, and rich, but a little shorter. We need to use them all in the right combination to make a beautiful finished wine. So now we will taste two examples of the finished wine.'

He lifted an unmarked open bottle that had been left on the upturned barrel that served as the tasting table and poured.

'So how old do you think it is?' he asked after we had observed and tasted.

'I really don't know,' said Dave.

'Don't even look at me,' said Chris. 'I'm just here to enjoy the ride.'

'Six years old?' I guessed.

Age would bring certain signs that help ascertain the vintage but telling two successive vintages apart many years later is often a matter of knowing the vintage conditions.

'Perhaps. It could be seven,' said Antoine. 'Mr Richard left it out and I'm not sure what it is. I'll go and check.'

'*Chapeau*,' he said on his return, a term that meant 'I lift my hat to you' and gave me a look of respect.

'How did you do that, Caro?' asked Chris.

'The colour and nose gave me an idea of the age range, then there was a clear fresh note to the wine I associate with the year of the early frost, the year we lost almost half our harvest,' I said. 'This year we had bad weather at flowering and lost almost half the Merlot. The weather gods like to shake it up a little.'

We all laughed. Antoine finished the visit with his favourite vintage, a wine that had won the *Coup de Cœur* award from the *Guide Hachette*, one of the most respected wine guides in France, alongside the hallowed Château Ausone, an estate that sold their top vintages for thousands of euro a bottle. Chris and Dave bought a couple of bottles, and we said *au revoir* to Antoine before driving carefully home at under 80 kilometres per hour on the biscuit tyre.

A couple of days later, after a hectic but successful harvest weekend and a tyre change, I said goodbye to the Drakes with tears in my eyes. In a short week, we had become part of their lives and they had become part of ours.

On their return home, Chris sent me photos of their celebration for her mum's ninetieth birthday in Hawaii, of Dave preparing the hall with one of our T-shirts on. Over the months Chris sent intermittent emails. Each one came at the right moment with the right message. I did her ten deep breaths each time I felt stress overcoming me and thought of her. After the breaths I felt renewed, calm and at ease.

CHAPTER 9

Cancer Up Close

I needed more than ten breaths to digest Sean's mum's news.

'The radiation was the start. I need chemotherapy now. When life knocks you to your knees it's not a bad time to start praying,' said Mum Feely in an email.

Mum Feely had been treated with radiation for a cancer spot on her lung. When she first told us about it, the cancer was an 'out there' idea, something like flu. It was bad but it would be fixed soon. Both our dads had had prostate cancer and recovered after radiation. I hadn't even looked up the details of what it meant to be radiated. I was a wimp when it came to medical issues. This was serious cancer – it needed chemotherapy. I had heard people talk about chemo but never experienced it in my immediate circle.

Mum Feely's email included a link to a website with a two-page summary of what chemotherapy was and the side effects it could create. I read through half a page and felt so horrified I couldn't continue. I closed it down, tears in my eyes. I felt sick that anyone should have to experience what I read. The side effects sounded worse than anything I could imagine. It was torture, not treatment.

That night on the phone to my mum, who trained as a nurse a lifetime before, I explained what I had read.

'Darling, they have to put all the side effects into documents like that. Not everyone will feel them,' said Mum.

She was trying to downplay it but I saw the look on the faces of chemotherapy survivors on documentaries I found online. It was a dark side of their lives that they could barely talk about. I didn't know enough about the 'treatment' but, as a medical simpleton, treating an illness with powerful poisons that also gave you cancer didn't make sense to me.

Mum Feely started the treatment. She had swelling, exhaustion, pain in her joints, nausea – almost every side effect that had been outlined, and in spades. She put a brave face on it and tried to be positive.

When I first met Sean's mum, Peta-Lynne, we had a slightly uneasy relationship – often the case between a girlfriend and a potential mother-in-law. We were very different. Peta-Lynne had trained as a nurse, like my mum. When her four kids were growing up, she was a stay-at-home mum for whom family was everything. Later she started a sideline business typing up recordings of court proceedings that allowed flexible hours and being at home for her family.

I was a career girl. I didn't even foresee myself having kids at that time. In spite of this discordance Peta-Lynne went out of her way to welcome me. She was mad about animals, and cats in particular. I painted a cat for her, and she gave it pride of place on the wall in the lounge.

In our first year on the farm Mum and Dad Feely visited us for six weeks. She and I started their long stay with a sense of unease. We hadn't seen each other in a while and I could tell that she didn't approve of how little cooking I did, the cleanliness of our house and the level of attention our daughters got. I could see her and my dad shaking their heads in shared disgust at what he called the 'Corridor of Crisis', aka our house, a normal house for a couple working long hours, with two kids under three – even without changing country, career, and language, or being in the middle of harvest.

A few weeks into their visit Sean chopped a third of his finger off on the harvest trailer. After that everything changed. We pulled together. I felt like we were seeing each other more clearly; for who we were and what we were doing right, rather than what we were doing 'wrong'. I felt very close to my parents-in-law after that baptism of fire.

Now Mum Feely was fighting for her life. The number of cancer lesions increased after the first go of chemo then reduced after the second. The oncologist felt it was worth it to continue. He upped the dose to a 'doublet therapy', a treatment of two chemicals, carboplatin and taxol. Even the names didn't sound good. They were administered by a slow drip that took five hours to feed into her body. Her hair started to fall out. She felt awful but she still sent upbeat messages to us and kept in regular touch with Sophia and Ellie, exchanging photos of cats and jokes. They found a wig maker.

'You should go for a visit,' I said to Sean. 'Perhaps waiting until next year is too long.'

We had been saving up for our family trip to South Africa and hoped to do it the following year for Mum and Dad Feely's fiftieth wedding anniversary.

'I think it's OK to wait,' said Sean. 'My mum is positive. She's going to get better.'

Sean's mum kept her emails coming. With the cancer lesions reducing, we felt upbeat about her progress.

For years we had been waiting for the final part of the financial aid for our tasting room and new Wine Lodge to be paid. I had jumped through so many administrative loops that I was ready to give up. For a period, my nightmares were about deadlines for signed copies in triplicate and incomprehensible letters in French. The last letter required another special trip to the accountant because the summary spreadsheet had rounded off the cents on some of the invoices listed. Given that the original signed invoices included the cents and were included in the same signed-in-triplicate package and that the rounding had no impact on the total value, it was a step too far for me.

I was ready to cry, 'Mercy! Keep the f'ing money!' when it hit the bank account. It was the green light we needed for the trip to South Africa, and for two building projects: the swimming pool and initial work on the exterior facades of the buildings. For the pool, we opted for a long rectangle that would look like a water feature rather than a classic swimming pool, and for saltwater rather than chlorine. I enjoyed planning and dreaming about the pool so much, I wondered if the reality could ever be as good as what I had imagined.

'Now staying at home in the summer will be like being on holiday,' said our pool constructor.

'Once our fourteen-hour workdays are done,' I replied and laughed.

'Oh, you'll find the time,' he said, and he was right.

We had chipped a metre square section of concrete off the house facade, so we knew there was stone underneath it, at least in part. Tomas, the mason that did the stonework on the Feely Wine Lodge, returned for this new restoration project. Each part whispered a little more of the history. The central section of the main house with a rounded cornice below the roof, was the oldest part, thought to be a 'lookout' built during the English rule of Aquitaine. Rounded cornices carved from stone were replaced by *genoise*, small bricks that look like a row of orange teeth, around the sixteenth century. Another part of the house was from the early 1700s, before the Revolution. We wished the stones could talk, although in a way they were, telling us via the methods they were cut and constructed, the era they were from.

'I think this double-storey part is older than you thought,' said Tomas as the work progressed. 'The stonework suggests sixteenth century. It looks like a fortress house, the sort they built during the religious wars. I can't wait to do the rest.'

I couldn't wait either, but we needed patience. We had to follow the cadence that time and budget allowed. Sean and I had decided that I couldn't go through another season without help. The reworked budget that included an apprentice salary meant the next phase of stonework had to take a back seat.

I waded through CVs and interviewed candidates, recalling Francine's advice on how important selecting the right person was. I asked two candidates to come back for second interviews and to do a few exercises to see how they handled some of the activities that were part of our daily fare. We made our selection, a young local woman who had done one year of university and wanted to change to tourism with an apprentice *alternance* contract. She accepted and we prepared for our first experience of hiring someone in France.

On the home front, it was the 'hungry gap' time of year; a moment when creating good food despite the dearth of ingredients, and doing outdoor activity despite the miserable weather, were necessary to stay sane. Christmas was long past, and spring seemed far, far away. I formulated a few tricks to keep my morale up.

First, I ate kale. Years before when I tasted kale for the first time it was 'No thanks for me'. We had a rule in our house that Sophia and Ellie were not allowed to say, 'That is disgusting', or similar, about food, so anything they didn't appreciate had become 'That's no thanks for me'. But kale cooked right tasted superb. Organic kale was also vitamin- and antioxidant-packed. Our *potager* was bursting with a purple cabbage kale that was delicious and helped us through the hungry gap.

Sophia, Ellie, and I noticed that even when it wasn't Sean's night he was inspired to cook on Wednesdays. He would spend hours in the kitchen. We were served sculptured towers of vegetables, delicious combinations, and imaginative impressions of single vegetables. We discovered kale three ways: as chips, with mashed potato and stir-fried. Wednesday couldn't come around quickly enough. We had spinach mousse, Jerusalem artichoke chips, hummus three ways – made with chickpeas in the classic way, with chickpeas and fists of fresh coriander leaves, and with beans instead of chickpeas. Sean's ideas were endless, and his gourmet plates were Michelin-star quality.

Sean had found the French version of *Top Chef*, the professional chef competition reality TV series. The three-hour show on Tuesday night meant he spent most of Wednesday thinking about what he would create, and we looked forward to it with our taste buds on high alert.

Sophia took to cooking. She turned out a round of potato soufflés worthy of a professional. Sean was impressed – and that was truly high praise. He was hard to please. Ellie started baking, making magnificent doughnuts, cheesecakes, hot cross buns. Sean was over the moon.

But no matter how high I set the bar on my cooking night, it wasn't good enough. I had to admit I didn't achieve the heights that Sean reached, but some nights I was impressed with my efforts, as were Sophia and Ellie. Sean's constant criticism was a thorn in my side. The next time Sean went off the deep end about the failure I had created I let rip.

'Sean, if you don't like my cooking and you don't like me anymore, we should just call a halt. I'm working as hard as I can. Sorry I don't have time to spend hours in the kitchen turning out wonders,' I said crossly.

'Just because you're busy doesn't mean you can behave like a monster and serve up slop. We're all busy,' he threw back.

'I don't know what you're staying with me for – all you do is criticise. You don't greet me in the morning; you don't say goodnight to me. I've had enough. We have to fix this, or I want out. I will not have it, Sean,' I said, getting more furious and upset with each word.

'Don't you talk to me about criticism,' he said. 'All you ever do is criticise me. You can't just throw a few roast vegetables together and call it dinner.' Sean's eyes flickered with anger.

'Stop fighting!' shouted Sophia. 'I can't take it anymore!' She started crying.

'Well, Sean should think about that next time he lambasts me and my efforts in the kitchen. I have had enough.'

I got up, slammed the door, and stormed out into the night, full of bitterness and angry tears. I wanted to run away and especially to get away from Sean. I didn't like who he was at that moment; I was losing respect for him. I felt like he was driving me away, that a wall had grown between us.

I had to find ways to cope with my new angry, violent self. I had always found winter tough, and that winter was worse.

We needed to get away. I found a last-minute special for four days at a spa in Ireland that was such a deal we could make it reality. We attached it to my planned marketing trip. Perhaps it would help plaster over the fissures in our relationship.

I took to drugs, adding organic hemp seeds to my morning muesli and to my home-made bread. Maybe it was my imagination, but hemp made me happier, perhaps not as happy as arriving in Ireland for our holiday.

'I love Dublin and I love Saussignac. They are so much better than Paris. There are no *gratte ciels*,' said Ellie. Skyscrapers barely existed in Dublin. At the time of our visit, the tallest building was Google Docks, 67 metres high.

'It's so friendly. It's not polluted,' said Sophia.

'Yes, for a city it's really not polluted,' said Ellie.

'And I love the sea,' said Sophia.

'And especially these moving stairs are great. You can even rest your case on the step above,' said Ellie, gazing in wonder at the magical escalator. The last time she had been on one was five years before, on a visit to Ireland when she turned four. Like our friend Thierry, when we visited Los Angeles in my second book 'Saving Our Skins', we were *ploucs*, country bumpkins, in awe of this high-tech cityscape.

'And laser water! *Mzzt, bzzt,*' said Sophia, referring to the sensor-operated water in the airport washroom we had just used.

Our tour of Ireland included some work but also play. We visited the people's park market in Dún Laoghaire. I spoke at a Grow It Yourself (GIY) group meeting. Markets and GIY were becoming more popular. Dublin fit like a well-worn glove. From there we took off into wild Ireland, with its layers of sea and sky and green pastures. It felt like home.

Driving from friends in County Meath down to County Cork, I watched the pastures through the car windows. Hills like a cardigan strewn with silver and lime bobbles and white-dot sheep filled the frame. A flying visit with Colm McCann, sommelier at Ballymaloe House Hotel and Ballymaloe Cookery School, was inspirational; the place buzzed with action and energy. I did a five-minute talk on Château Feely and organic and biodynamic wine to the cookery-school class then we raced on to Cork city for a talk and tasting at a chic wine bar, L'Atitude 51.

Mary Pawle, our wine importer and friend, took me on a tour to meet the people that stocked our wines. She introduced me to a pal that was doing a PhD on the food and wine in James Joyce's *Ulysses* and living in a funky apartment in the heart of the city. I felt a flash of envy for the freedom of her single student life.

The swans near Clonakilty sat between sea and river on beach sand tufted with grass; a rugged, beautiful scene. Seascape everywhere. Inchydoney Spa offered us aperitifs in a luxurious lounge with floor-to-ceiling panoramic views of the sea. We felt like royalty.

Our apartment's expansive windows looked on to infinite wild Atlantic. I opened the doors and felt the sound of it pouring through me. Sophia, Ellie and Sean went on to the balcony, leaned out and sucked in the salty sea air and crashing waves. Ellie was in my gold bowling shoes. I had a strange sensation like I was looking into my past and my future.

Then the rain was lashing so hard we closed the doors, and the glass became a mass of liquid dots moving in a crazy dance. In Cork city someone had recommended an app that predicted exactly when the next shower would come and go. The rain stopped in eight minutes and the sun came out. I moved from one side of the sofa to the other to escape the glare off the sea.

'It's such a beautiful day it's a crime not to be out there,' I said.

'We're going to the lounge for the Wi-Fi and then to the spa,' said Ellie.

'OK, Papa can go with you. I want to go for a long walk,' I said.

'I didn't say I wanted to go to the spa,' said Sean.

'OK, I'll go for a quick walk and be back to catch the last half hour of the kids' session in the spa,' I said.

'Good. See you at eleven thirty so,' said Sean.

'No, midday,' I said.

They scrummaged out of the door, electronic devices in hand, on a mission to find the library lounge where the heavenly Wi-Fi was.

A tiny chocolate-brown bird perched on the balcony railing for a second then flew off. I put the washing on and prepared to go. As I picked up the keys, the bright sun that had been blinding seconds before disappeared behind a black storm cloud. The wind thrashed; the rain lashed, then it snowed. I took a photo of the cars covered in snow in case it was gone by the time my family emerged from the main hotel and they didn't believe me. I tidied my suitcase into neat piles of shirts and trousers. I took the rubbish out to the bins outside, my face stinging in the freezing rain. It was still too wet. I went back inside and stared out of the window, wishing the rain away. It went. I felt a sense of power commanding the weather like that.

Then I was out of the door in my runners and rain gear. I raced along the car park and down the long set of concrete stairs, passing one soul coming back well soaked. The beach was empty. High on the dune his tracks were white, each footprint filled with snow. I ran down the beach, singing and laughing into the wind. The blue sky was clear save for a seagull crying lonesomely. Solid sand then soft sand. I began to recognise the colour codes to avoid sinking and tracked along the hard sections.

At the end of the strand, I felt the bracing wind pick up a notch, and saw an ominous black cloud in the distance. I turned and raced back, the wind carrying me, flying and singing with the sun bright in my face and the cold darkness rolling in behind me.

Faster and faster I ran. Almost out of breath, I raced up the steps two by two and back across the car park. The first splats hit my back as I took the corner on to the concrete pavement of the apartments. I scrambled to get the key in the door and was inside gasping as the fury hit. It was so dark I needed lights on even though it was nearly midday. I did a few stretches to calm down and watched the grey waves swirling under the charcoal sky. Then I grabbed my swimsuit and ran the gauntlet to the main hotel to take Sophia and Ellie to the spa.

Our holiday was so good I swore we had to take more time off. But when we returned home, we were quickly back into long days and thoughts of holidays disappeared like the snow tracks had on the beach. I sorted through the emails received while I was away. I replied to some while we were away, but I didn't get to everything. I waded back and saw an email from FranceAgriMer asking for an additional document over and above those already requested as part of our application for state aid for modernising parts of our winery. It ended with: '*Sans retour de votre part en date du 27/02, votre dossier se verra automatiquement rejeté*' - 'Without your reply before 27/02 your file will be automatically rejected'. We had missed the deadline by two days. I felt a cold sweat break out. The email had arrived 15 minutes after we left for our week away. It was Sunday morning, the last day of our 'holiday', and I spent it in a total panic.

'We mustn't apply for aid anymore,' I said to Sean. 'I can't take the stress.'

'What? That would be madness. If everyone else is doing it and we don't, how can we compete? I know it's a pain to do but it has helped us enormously. Look at the current projects, we wouldn't be doing them without the aid payments that just came in.'

I called first thing on Monday and discovered that my contact was away on holiday until Thursday. A colleague of hers called me back and within hours everything was resolved. I had to learn to be Zen, my day of panic had contributed nothing except unnecessary suffering for me.

Sean and I continued to drift apart, barely acknowledging each other except for business affairs. I was short-tempered and edgy. My disrupted sleep and dreams of dying continued. The hot flushes got worse. Sometimes I felt like I was burning up from the inside. Perimenopause was bad and I felt like no one was talking about it. I searched online and found more articles that confirmed what I was experiencing. It proved that some people were talking about it, but mainstream media wasn't. It remained a taboo subject.

Worry about Mum Feely churned in the back of our minds. She appeared to be making progress, but chemo's side effects were terrible – at least as bad as the article I couldn't bear to finish. It was like voluntary torture, but she hadn't been given any other options.

The cranes passed over. There was a feeling of freedom in the cold air and blue sky. They called way up high, so far up they were almost invisible. Black spots set in great Vs across the sky, V upon V, upon V, upon V. They announced the change of seasons, our connection to the earth, the power of instinct. I felt the earth turning, the return of the sun.

CHAPTER 10

Language and Philosophic Challenges

'**M**adame Feely?' said a voice on the phone.

'*Oui.*'

'Mr Vellami, Vellami *méthode traditionelle.*'

I was surprised to receive a phone call from the *patron*, the boss; I had only ever spoken to his salesperson. Over the years we had had great success with our sparkling *méthode traditionelle* (MT), a favourite with clients and visitors, and a special favourite with Rosie, our Zimbabwean friend, that attended my parent's Golden wedding. It was dry and crisp with citrus and green apple aromas, and a yeasty, biscuity note; easy to see why she mistook it for Champagne. Each year we made about 600 bottles. Once the fermentation was finished and the wine was stable, we gave it to Vellami, a service provider that did the *méthode traditionelle* – the fermentation in the bottle,

the same method that creates the bubbles in Champagne –
for us. Each year we sold out before the next batch arrived.
We were considering making double to meet the demand.
I had been chasing them for weeks for the delivery of our
latest batch and to talk about the next vintage.

'I'm very sorry but we have lost our organic label,' he
said.

'What do you mean 'lost the label'?' I asked. 'We really
need that wine. We've been sold out for months and I've
promised it to many people.'

'We have your wine, don't worry. We can deliver next
week. But we have to label without the organic logo.'

'Why?' I asked, my brain trying to grasp what he was on
about.

'Our processes weren't controlled enough between
bottling an organic lot and a non-organic lot. When we
changed from one to the other there was a chance that
a tiny bit of non-organic got into the lot and vice versa,'
replied Vellami.

'But is it still our specific lot? Our wine?' I asked.

'Absolutely,' he replied.

'So it's an administrative issue about your changeover
controls?' I asked.

'Yes, exactly,' he said.

Organic certification controls had been tightened. The
local bakery stopped doing organic baguettes because the
controls were too strict. They had to completely clean
the kitchen each time they did an organic lot in case a
little chemically farmed flour got in via a floured surface.
It wasn't economic for them to spend hours cleaning
down the kitchen given the volume of organic they were
producing. In the local supermarket they stopped cutting

the organic loaves because the cutting machine had to be dedicated to organic to be sure that a few crumbs of non-organic bread didn't get in. I could see where these rules were coming from but on the other hand, it was decreasing supply, and decreasing demand for organic. Busy people preferred pre-sliced bread, and some would select non-organic as a result. It sounded like the Vellami situation was a similar case of the tightening of the process rules.

Our sparkling was the only wine that left the property before it went into a bottle and with this crisis I saw the risks involved in that. With the rest of our wine range every process from pruning to bottling had our fingerprints on it. I could see the value in our artisanal methods.

'What will you do for us? Not having the organic label decreases the value of the wine. It's a serious issue,' I said.

'We won't charge you anything more for the service. We'll keep your deposit, but you won't have to pay the balance,' he said.

'OK,' I said, digesting the news and too surprised by the whole affair to negotiate.

'We will deliver next week *alors*,' he said.

'Yes, please deliver as quickly as possible. We really need our wine.'

I felt gutted about the sparkling losing its organic label but also pleased that organic was so carefully protected in Europe. It was reassuring in a world of food rocked by scandals. The fraud of horsemeat sold as beef was still reverberating around the nation's radio stations, a classic example of industrial food production gone wrong.

The food industry was also rife with loose terms. 'Irish smoked salmon' and 'smoked Irish salmon' were totally different. The first was merely smoked in Ireland; the second was Irish salmon. Terms like 'natural', 'farm-fresh' and 'sustainable' had been hijacked by the large-scale food industry and offered no meaning whatsoever. Someone shopping for their family needed to have hours to read each label and a PhD in food science to decipher them. It was part of the reason why if we did have to go food shopping we typically bought exclusively from local organic shops. Their ethos meant that I didn't need to read every label for its fine details; I didn't have time. Economic *and* organic were becoming possible in France. Our local organic shop offered bulk bins of core products that were our staples. They often had local, organic, in-season fruit at a lower cost than the same chemically farmed fruit in the supermarket.

As Vellami had promised, we took delivery of our Feely Sparkling Brut MT a week later. We were relieved it tasted like ours. We wouldn't risk another batch with them. I searched for a new MT service provider, someone who specialised in organic rather than someone who did organic as a sideline. Tighter regulations also meant our annual bottling was even more complicated than when we started. Our labels had to be checked by three different parties and we had nine references.

'I'm dreaming about the bottling,' I said to Sean as we drank our morning tea.

'I know,' he replied. 'It's déjà vu. You rolled over and said "corks, labels, capsules" in a panicked voice in the middle of the night. You did the same thing a few years ago.'

It was a premonition. An email arrived saying the labels still weren't right – there had been yet another administrative rejection by Ecocert, our organic certifier.

I called our label provider back for the fifth time and explained that the new law required the mention of Agriculture France below the sign Ecocert FR-BIO-01. He sent the new label back with it above. There wasn't a lot of difference between *dessous* and *dessus* – it was in the lips, and mine had failed.

It wasn't only language that I found disconcerting. I dropped a friend at Bordeaux airport and was stuck on the ring road of Bordeaux in what felt like a giant car park. It gave me time to reflect on many things, including how grateful I was that we did not face city traffic every day. It also gave me time to listen to the radio.

There were two key topics of discussion. The first was a ceiling on rents in Paris. The French government had set band limits for rents by *arrondissement* or district. For me the obvious negative effect was a slow pull to the bottom; there would be no incentive to renovate or invest. When that topic was exhausted the radio host moved on to a ferry company that was about to close because it was not making any profit. A Scandinavian company had offered to purchase it, but the employees had voted against the purchase. In essence they preferred that the business closed, and they lost their jobs than that they were purchased and helped to become more competitive, thereby securing their jobs. I felt like Alice in Wonderland.

When I reached home after three hours of driving, having listened to more radio than was good for me, there was barely time to shower before going to Thierry and Isabelle Daulhiac, winegrower friends in Razac-de-Saussignac, for dinner.

The table was set in their *cuisine d'été*, their summer kitchen. It was a traditional lean-to, with Roman tiles on the roof, a stone wall at the back, with the barbecue built into the wall and a counter running to the right providing preparation surface and a small sink. Thierry was good with his hands. Along with his day job of being a *vigneron*, he offered tool-engineering advice to a vineyard equipment manufacturer in Germany and could turn his skills to building work too. They had recently finished a major renovation of their house, transforming it into an ecological haven. In winter wood-fired heating ran under their tiled floor and the warmth was kept in by hemp insulation on the walls. They had created a large open plan living, cooking, eating space rather than separate rooms. The summer kitchen was a recent addition.

'We need one like this,' said Sean, admiring the set-up.

'It's true – in summer, we use it a lot. We live outside, in fact,' said Thierry. 'Especially when it's as hot as last summer.'

Isabelle arrived with aperitifs and a bottle of wine and we settled into outdoor sofas. Opposite us were two hammocks: one for lying in and one that was like a swing seat. Sophia and Ellie were attracted to them like magnets.

'Hey, girls, what about a drink?' asked Isabelle. 'Coke? Fruit juice?'

'Coke,' they replied.

'Fruit juice,' I said, jumping in. I avoided sodas like the plague. They were bad for health and bad for the planet.

Sophia and Ellie glared at me.

'*Quoi de neuf?*' said Thierry. 'What's new *chez* Feely?'

'Ah, you know, twiddling our thumbs,' said Sean.

He and Thierry laughed. They were entering the busiest time for the vineyard. Vegetal growth was motoring towards its peak, creating the need for mowing, weeding and trimming. Potential dangers of pests and diseases were also gathering pace, so spray treatments were required even in organic winegrowing – but these were natural contact sprays rather than systemic.

'I was in Bordeaux today – that's why we're late,' I said. 'Traffic hell.'

'Me too!' said Isabelle. 'What a nightmare. An hour and a half for what should take ten minutes.'

'It gave me time to listen to the radio, which was more scary than the traffic. What are they thinking with fixing rents in Paris?' I asked.

'Oh no, I find it a good thing. It's time they stopped the rents from going stratospheric. Normal people can't afford to live in the city anymore,' said Isabelle.

'But, Isabelle, it means that people have no incentive to renovate their apartments. Everything will be pulled to the bottom. Bad areas with run-down apartments will stay run-down. Fewer investors will make apartments available for rent.'

'Oh no, I am not in agreement. We have to stop the rich owners from gouging normal people who need a place to live near their work.'

'But if we leave the market to be free then people can choose to renovate or not and can choose the price they want to charge, and renters are free to choose. If it gets too expensive people will move to less expensive areas and so on. The rents reflect the cost of the property too; it's based on availability and demand. We can't legislate this – it's economic reality.'

'No, absolutely not. We cannot leave students and workers to be the ones to do the long-distance travel to their study or workplace. We need to have local places where they can afford to live.'

Isabelle was the economics teacher at the local agricultural college. It was a full-time job, but she had a second job helping Thierry with their vineyard administration. I tried to see where Isabelle was coming from, but I was too much of a free marketeer. I could see too many bad things coming out of too much legislation. We needed freedom of choice that enabled creativity and rejuvenation. The discussion was getting heated.

'I can see that Caro is coming from one side and Isabelle is coming from another. I think you're both right in some ways, but I don't think we'll be able to get you to agree so let's eat and drink,' said Thierry, acting the diplomat.

We all laughed. We probably would never agree but hearing Isabelle's arguments did make me reflect on the other side of the story.

Thierry raised his glass in a toast. '*Santé!* To your health!'

We clinked glasses.

Isabelle's cooking prowess was legendary. She could turn out a gourmet dinner while organising their sons' homework, solving the business's marketing and administrative problems, and planning Thierry and his part-time employee's workdays. She was a superwoman. I knew Sean wished I was as gifted. We moved from a luscious salad with walnuts and feta to duck breast that Thierry had cooked on the outside barbecue.

'I am not good,' said Thierry.

'*Au contraire*, this is some of the best duck I've ever had,' I said after taking a forkful.

'How do you do it?' asked Sean, eager to pick up new tricks.

'Well, Isabelle does it. I just put it on the barbecue,' replied Thierry.

'In fact, it's really easy,' said Isabelle. 'I slice it and marinade it then Thierry puts it on to the barbecue for a very short time.'

'So the marinade is "*vin et aile*"?' I said.

Sophia and Ellie laughed, and I knew I had made a faux pas.

'*Vin et ail*,' corrected Isabelle.

'Wine and wing' wasn't quite the same as 'wine and garlic'. The cooking technique was one we hadn't tried and it worked a charm. This was one to add to our duck recipes. We loved to barbecue down near Sean's prolific *potager*.

'Are you still running?' asked Isabelle.

'No, I twisted my *chenille* a week or so ago,' I replied.

Sophia and Ellie burst out laughing again. They tried to be discreet but there was no covering it up.

'*Cheville*,' corrected Isabelle, laughing too.

I was providing the entertainment for the night.

'*La chenille, la chenille, la chenille,*' chanted Thierry, overhearing and cutting away from his discussion with Sean. 'Do you know the tradition of dancing the caterpillar at French weddings?'

He started acting out the caterpillar dance.

We nodded, already laughing at his rendition.

'Isabelle didn't want it at ours. It was too *plouc* for her. She had a horror of it. We told the DJ that we categorically didn't want it; that the music he played must not even encourage thoughts of the caterpillar dance. But our friends bribed the DJ to play the caterpillar music and they all started dancing it at full speed. We were forced to join in. Sorry, my beloved Isabelle, what can I say? You married a *plouc*.'

Thierry was hilarious when he got going with his stories.

'Even more so now we are *bio, hé, ma chérie*?' he said. 'Isabelle is shocked. Why do our organic advisers have to look so organic? The long hair, the dreadlocks, the beards, clothes that haven't been washed in a few days. She is worried I will start to look like that. That will be worse than dancing the *chenille, hé, chérie*?'

Picturing Thierry transformed into a bearded dread-head; Isabelle was laughing so much she couldn't answer – she just nodded.

'Now, on to more serious subjects,' she said, gaining control of herself. 'We're looking for extra people for my Thursday yoga class. Do you know of anyone that might want to join us?'

'I would love to try it,' I said. 'I've been looking for a yoga class that can fit my schedule. When is it?'

'Thursday evening. We can go together if you like. Sharing transport is better for the planet and more fun. Meet me in front of the Relais de Monestier the first Thursday in September and you can try a session to see if you like it.'

'It's a date.'

With one chance exchange I found my yoga session. Perhaps it would help me with the difficult passage through perimenopause.

I checked the weather forecast before washing clothes. For ecological and financial reasons, I preferred to hang rather than use the drier. At first it seemed like a nasty chore. Slowly my attitude changed. Now I enjoyed it. It was methodical, melodic. It was a service to those I loved.

'Peg one side on to the line. Take the other side and peg it on. Bend, take the next item, peg it with the same peg as the first, then take a new peg for the other side, and so on,' I said, showing Ellie.

We worked steadily together, filling the four strands of wire that ran the 12-metre length of the *potager*. As we worked, the Dordogne Valley changed with the rising sun; the plum trees, vines and forests dressed in shimmering greens, their peak-season splendour. The Merlot vines closest to us were lime-green brilliant; in a few weeks their leaves would be dark green, and the bunches of grapes would change from green to purple.

The last items were crocheted blankets made by my grandmothers. We watched the multicoloured squares dancing like stained-glass windows in the bright sun for a moment. Both my grandmothers had passed on, but I felt their love in these beautiful things handcrafted from wool scraps so long ago. In the twenty-first century it was much easier to buy a synthetic blanket. Both my grans rarely sat with nothing to do. Whether chatting over tea or watching television, their hands were busy with something for family or friends.

We finished in time to walk up for Ellie's school bus, chatting and singing en route, enjoying being together. I loved our shared walks up and down each day; they were treasured moments. Sophia and Ellie hadn't taken to the idea of walking or cycling to begin with. Even though it was only a kilometre, it was tempting to get into a lump of metal and be propelled by fossil fuel, especially first thing in the morning. I bribed them with money, paying the equivalent of what we saved in fuel by not driving. It was the incentive required to start doing it grumpily. Now we walked even when there was a little rain and enjoyed it; it had become a habit.

That evening I walked up to meet Sophia, who had started high school and was on a different bus timetable to Ellie. I missed walking together as a threesome but going up and back to Saussignac with Sophia and with Ellie was good for my fitness and for Dora, plus it gave me an opportunity to talk to them individually.

'So what have you and Papa been up to?' asked Sophia.

'I'm finishing off a book about wine for my publisher,' I said.

'Oh, that's good. You know, I'm very proud of you for writing books.'

'Thank you, Sophia. I appreciate your compliment,' I said.

'And Papa?' asked Sophia.

'He's been working in the vineyard most of the day.'

'It's a bit of a waste of his education,' said Sophia. 'You don't need to go to school to work in the vines.'

'*Au contraire,*' I responded. 'Working with living things and creating great wine requires wisdom, art, science, and instinct. Where did you get that idea?'

'At school.'

'People working creatively with their hands and nature are highly skilled. They should be honoured and appreciated as much as bureaucrats, lawyers, or engineers.'

Our urban world was getting further and further from nature. In French school there was no 'nature' education and little encouragement to take risks; if the kids weren't sure their answer was correct, they wouldn't try to answer. A significant school reform programme was announced, part of it an effort to correct this recognised problem. The teachers' unions took up strike action to counter it. The programme was a step forward for the education system, but any change was systematically rejected. We loved so many things about France – the history, the food, the culture, the markets – things that ironically had been preserved by an unwillingness to change.

The following day it was barely light when Sophia tore round the corner on her bike and passed my office window. Her teachers were on strike, and she and her friend Julie wanted to do something useful with their day, so they offered to help Olga, the chef at Saussignac school, the local primary establishment, which wasn't on strike that day. I was impressed with their idea and her motivation to get up and be in Saussignac for 7.30 a.m. when she could have been cosy in bed.

I ran outside and yelled, 'Put your hat on!'

'I don't want a hat,' shouted Sophia. She paused and looked back.

'You have to wear a hat,' I shouted.

'No! I don't want to!' she shouted back, then took off again.

'Stop!' I yelled.

'I'm going to be late. I'm going.'

'No, Sophia. You wait there. I'll get it for you.'

'I don't want it,' she shouted. She pedalled away again.

'Sophia! You stop right there! You do not speak to me like this!' I yelled. 'You're not going anywhere! You get off that bike! You're going to the naughty corner!'

In my angry perimenopausal mania I was resorting to techniques that would have worked when she was four years old, except I never needed them. She was such an angel; she always listened. She stopped and looked at me aghast. I realised how stupid I sounded.

'Stop right there,' I said. 'You're not going anywhere without your helmet.'

I ran to the shed, found the helmet and raced back.

She grabbed it from me with a look of fury mingled with astonishment.

'I thought you meant my woolly hat. I didn't realise you were talking about a helmet. I didn't want to wear the woolly hat.'

She raced off. The broken telephone was at work again. Only this time in English.

Sean signed Sophia and Ellie up to a programme that would give them A-level English by the end of their French schooling and thereby offer them a wider choice of tertiary education. Perhaps it would help us to understand each other better too.

Spring was almost over. We had successfully bottled our latest vintages. Demand for our accommodation, wine school and visits kept growing and promised to stretch me to the boundaries of my capability. I could see fourteen-hour days shimmering in my future and hoped that our apprentice, due to start in a few weeks, and my planned yoga session with Isabelle would help me stay sane.

CHAPTER 11

Powerful Herbs and Dancing Bees

I looked to our garden for solutions to ease the ratty, sleep-deprived monster I had become. Most pharmaceuticals started out as medicines made from plants. Having a herb garden outside was like having a natural pharmacy available 24/7. It would do me good to remember Hippocrates advice to '*let food be thy medicine and medicine be thy food*'.

Lavender is a great soother. It calms, reduces stress, improves sleep, and soothes inflammation in the body. I found that drinking a *tisane* – infusion - made of lavender calmed my nerves. Merely running my hand over lavender plants and inhaling the aroma lifted my mood. But I read that it wasn't a good idea to drink lavender tea for two weeks before surgery since it could slow down your central nervous system. These were powerful plants to be treated with respect.

I often found the ancient song 'Parsley, Sage, Rosemary and Thyme' coming naturally to my lips as I picked herbs in the garden. These four famous herbs are culinary but also medicinal. The first one, parsley, lifts buttery scrambled egg on toast from a casual supper to a heavenly feast, especially when paired with Feely *Générosité* barrel-aged white. Our main *potager* parsley often went to seed in the summer heat but the parsley that had self-seeded into crevices along the north-facing winery wall thrived all year round. They knew where was best for them.

Another parsley classic we loved was tabbouleh, a couscous salad packed with this magic herb and other bits that had become a summer staple for us. Parsley provides vitamins K, C and A, folic acid and iron in good levels, is a great cleanser and has been popular for more than 2,000 years – in fact, it was used medicinally before being used in cooking.

The second herb in the song, sage, was another favourite. It grew like a weed in our first *potager* on the hot plateau where the swimming pool now had pride of place. After years of dreaming, it was a reality. Ad, our friend from Holland who, with his wife Lijda, had been part of our farm's story since the beginning, arrived to build the iron fence for our new swimming pool. No ordinary fence would do; it would be a beautiful handmade fence. Ad, the bionic man, was as fit as ever. He lifted lengths of metal that I couldn't even drag, and barely broke a sweat. At the end of a hard week weight-lifting metalwork he rode his bike to Sainte-Foy-la-Grande to relax.

Before taking off on his cycle ride one evening, Ad helped me unload two boxes of live chickens. We had decided we couldn't wait any longer and had purchased a selection: two white, two brown and two with beautiful high-sheen black feathers. They were different breeds to our original chickens, which had been a classic French laying breed with bare necks. I was tired of explaining that bare necks did not mean they were sick, so these new chickens had thick and lustrous feathers around theirs. The sun was shining bright; lime-green leaves created dappled shade from the afternoon sun. We let the chickens out in the run and they immediately started scratching like it was home.

'Chicken paradise,' said Ad.

'It is,' I replied. 'I love the black ones – that beautiful sheen.'

We made sure the chickens had settled and Ad went for his bike ride. Then we took a Friday night break to the pizzeria in Gardonne. When we returned the chickens were happily roosting in trees and not in the henhouse. Our previous chickens had roamed free; we didn't close them in at night and we never had a problem.

This time not so: the next morning we found chicken hell. A fox had got in and both black sheen hens and one of the whites were gone. The feisty brown chickens had made it – there was no messing with them. I felt sad and Sean felt culpable. We had never seen foxes close to the houses at the top of the hill. From then on, we closed our chickens into the henhouse religiously.

Now the plateau sage was replaced by a pool but we had transferred some plants to the pots in the courtyard and to the new *potager* so we could continue to enjoy the herb.

The official name of sage, *Salvia officinalis*, originates from the Latin word *salvare*, 'to be saved'. It is a miracle herb, preserving and helping memory - I needed to eat more - and aiding digestion. In winter I loved to pick it fresh and serve it with honey as a *tisane*. It is recommended as an anti-inflammatory and to combat arthritis, asthma, and Alzheimer's. It is also an excellent source of vitamin K.

Before fridges sage was used to preserve meat as it is a powerful antioxidant. In the seventeenth century it was so sought after the Chinese traded three bushels of dried tea for one bushel of dried sage from the Dutch. When it came to cooking, sage suited sweet and sour. The sage and Saussignac jelly I made brought cold meats and cheeses to life. With Roquefort cheese it was heaven.

The third herb in the song, rosemary, was delicious in winter served with aubergines, potatoes, lamb, duck – actually, most things. I loved to throw sprigs into my jams to give them a hint of something unexpected. But I discovered it was useful beyond cooking; the leaves offered calcium, iron, and vitamin B6, and a branch on my clothesline kept ants away. It is also a medicinal herb for memory and concentration and has anti-cancer and anti-inflammatory properties. Chopped fine and mixed with garlic and a little salt, sprinkled and baked on polenta, it was a delicious snack.

Rosemary contains carnosol, a potential cancer-preventing chemical. Research shows it inhibits the growth of breast tumours in studies of rats. Rosemary also helps lift your morale, relieves pain - including migraines, aids digestion, and has antibacterial properties. It can be used as breath freshener and to stimulate hair growth.

Rosemary can do well in and out of pots, and in the right conditions will grow into a large shrub with sky blue flowers. Researchers put the exceptional longevity of an Italian seaside village, Acciaroli, down to rosemary, anchovies, and outdoor living. I was pleased to see the researchers noted that these amazing people - in a village of 2,000 inhabitants, more than 300 were 100 years plus - were not shy of enjoying a glass of wine either.

The last in the song, thyme, was my favourite herb to kill a sore throat. The instant I felt one creeping up, I put a great bunch of thyme in a cup and poured hot water over it. A few minutes later, when it had cooled and extracted the benefits from the herb, I added a large teaspoon of honey and a drop of organic lemon juice. It was a magic pick-me-up.

Thyme kills off bacterial throat infections and helps decrease the oxidation and degradation of everything from sunflower oil to cheese. It is also an excellent source of vitamin C, a very good source of vitamin A, and a good source of iron, manganese, fibre and copper. But most of all, it is delicious. I sprinkled thyme on fresh tomatoes with a little oil and vinegar for a taste sensation or grilled it on tomato and goat's cheese toasts. Like rosemary, thyme can do well in or out of pots, in the right conditions.

The famous four were staples for us and we always had a few thriving bushes. Growing herbs gave me cooking inspiration. It was also the best way to be sure the herbs had been grown in a healthy fashion. In the new half-shaded vegetable garden, herbs like borage, coriander, and basil, were thriving at last. They were a tonic for us but also for the pollinators. The borage hummed like a propeller aeroplane about to take off it was so packed with bees, some recently received from a local beekeeper, Mr Patriarcha.

'If you don't use the smoker the bees will take Sean from here to Monestier,' he said, his greying head bent over his *forgon* - utility vehicle - parked in our courtyard.

'We were hoping to work more naturally and to avoid smoking the bees,' I said.

He laughed heartily. 'You must respect the bees but smoking doesn't harm them. Look at this beautiful mix – it is lavandin granules, lavender and pine needles,' he said, lifting the lid off a metal container in the back of his van.

I dipped my head inside and felt like I was stepping into a warm, relaxing bath.

Mr Patriarcha closed his eyes and leaned back like he was going into a trance.

'You see, that's what it does to the bees too – it calms them, relaxes them – so we can do the work we need to do,' he said dreamily.

Mr Patriarcha had delivered our hives earlier in the spring. At the Christmas market five months earlier, he announced that he was winding down his activity in order to retire and looking to sell most of his hives. We bought two.

The bees appeared to have settled into their new home. On this, his second visit, he checked on them and offered advice on how to manage them. As the months progressed, we learned about the bees, and I felt a whole new level of respect for each teaspoon of honey I ate. They tapped around 4,400 flowers and flew about 175 kilometres to make 1 gram of honey.

The bees were giving a clear early warning to the human race. They were dying in hordes, with 'colony collapse disorder' sounding the alarm about the environmental degradation caused by pesticides. In places like California, the almond and fruit farmers paid fortunes to bring bees from the other side of the USA and even flew them in from Australia because their own populations had been so decimated.

Bees have a sophisticated society and work together for the good of the hive. They are the ultimate socialists. They do a dance at the hive entrance to tell the other bees where to find the best flowers, giving the GPS coordinates in bee-speak and saving time on searching and unnecessary flying. This is where the systemic pesticides, particularly a relatively new type called nicotinoids, are most dangerous. They work on the bees' nervous system and impact the bees' ability to remember where flowers are located and how to find their way home. Some are shown to not kill bees directly but, by impacting their ability to forage for nectar, to remember where flowers are located, and to find their way home, they destroy the bees.

With research showing a direct impact on the bees' nervous system, these kinds of insecticides may also be part of the reason for massive increases in nervous system disorders, like Alzheimer's - up 500 percent according to a recent study - and Parkinson's, among humans. It is not possible to wash systemic pesticides off fruit and vegetables, so eating certified organic or healthily homegrown, is the only way to avoid carcinogenic, nervous-system- and endocrine-disrupting chemicals getting into your body.

We learned that a key difference between organic and biodynamic honey was that organic beekeepers could still take all the honey, as long as they provided the bees with an organic certified version of the sugar syrup offered as replacement. With biodynamic honey, the beekeeper had to leave enough of the bees' own honey for them to survive the winter. The bees' honey was packed with immunity boosters, making it worth far more than the calorie value. With their real honey the hive avoided many of the health problems that were damaging bee populations. But it was more expensive than the honey – even the organic one – I found on the shelf in the supermarket. Now we knew the work that went into the honey – for the bees, let alone the beekeeper – we knew the price was justified.

Things were changing in other parts of the farm thanks to the bees. We left the ivy in the vineyard because along with biodiversity, the ivy offered bees flowers and hence pollen in early winter – one of the few plants that did. Ivy isn't a parasite – it climbs, so it doesn't harm the vine.

Through the beekeeping experience we learned that all honey, like wine, was not the same. They reflected their *terroir*. We tasted honey from bees collecting pollen from lavender, sunflowers, spring flowers, summer flowers, chestnut forests, and found they all had their unique flavour, a real sense of where they were from. Like some wine, some honeys were not as wholesome as you might think. Jars marketed as honey had even been found to contain no honey at all, just corn syrup.

Our apprentice Sandrine started her trial period with us. I asked her if she wanted to taste the honey from Mr Patriarcha.

'No thanks. I don't like honey,' she replied.

'Why not try a little? This local honey might be different to what you have had,' I said.

She tasted.

'Hmmm. You are right. It's great. It doesn't taste like the honey I've had before. I really like it,' she said.

'I read that three quarters of the "honey" sold in the world is not honey,' I said. 'It's corn syrup dressed up as honey, or honey laced with corn syrup.'

'I saw a television show about that,' she said. 'That must be why I didn't like the honey I had before. I will send you the link.'

'Thanks, Sandrine, I would appreciate that,' I said.

Sometimes canny labelling leads to misunderstanding and other times it's plain fraud. Research points to the health dangers of corn syrup while the health-giving properties of honey are legendary. It can even give truffles some competition as an aphrodisiac. Hippocrates apparently prescribed honey for sexual vigour. Honey contains boron, which helps regulate hormone levels and nitric oxide, which helps increase blood flow during arousal.

Sandrine was keen and appeared to be embracing our organic perspective even though she had not arrived with that philosophy. Training her with the season already in full swing added to my stress although I knew it was necessary. I shoehorned training time into already extended days. At the end of another long day, I ran out of the tasting room to cross the courtyard and flew across the gravel again. This time it was worse. My toes, knees, hands, and chin were bleeding, and I had a bump on my forehead I had come down so hard. I washed and disinfected my grazes then sat down, my head spinning. I had to slow down and get a grip. I felt like I was on the cusp of a nervous breakdown.

But as the days progressed things got better. The initial extra stress was worth it, and Sandrine became a lifesaver for me. She needed guidance but she was keen. Wine sales were going well and growing; more wine lovers visited the property each season and our mailing list grew. Sandrine learned to sell wine at the château door and to fulfil internet orders. She followed me on visits, and we set a target for her to be comfortable doing the half-day visits at our farm on her own by the end of the season. The time invested would really pay off the following summer when she would know the ropes and be able to make a serious contribution. Our first foray into employment in France was working out.

While direct sales were flying, trade sales were not. The price of our wines had gone up in line with the increasing quality and cost increases. Trade clients were more price-sensitive than direct clients who tasted and bought based on quality not price. We had to develop trade sales that would help us to sell more wine direct from the farm. I made a list of the top restaurants in the region, the ones we most wanted to be in, and talked through them with Sandrine. I hoped that having a French person to represent us would help with restaurant sales and that would in turn bring us more clients in the season.

'We must target these places with our wines, especially the Michelin-star restaurants,' I said. 'We're already on La Tour des Vents' wine list. I want to be on the wine list of Le Vieux Logis in Trémolat. I've read that it's the best restaurant in the Dordogne.'

'How will we do it?' asked Sandrine.

'We'll have to research as much as we can about them then see if we can meet the sommelier. We're too busy now. It's a project for winter.'

Our restaurant list was put on the back burner. With the tourist season well under way we couldn't spend time away from the property. We had reached a point where we regularly sold out of our whites and our top reds before the next bottling, but we still had extra volume of our everyday Merlot red wine. We joined a newly conceived grouping of organic growers set up to sell the growing volume of bulk organic wine available in the region, hoping it would be a channel to sell our excess. France had gone from 1 percent of the vineyards certified organic when we arrived ten years before, to almost 8 percent.

More organic farmers represented potential for the region. State aid was promised for the grouping, enough to fund a salesperson, stands at wine fairs and the development of a brand. As a foreigner and relative newcomer, I sat quietly on the side watching the meetings and reading the emails. An uneasy feeling grew with each exchange.

The president of the management body and the newly appointed salesperson created a presentation that said we shouldn't communicate about organic because their research said, 'No one wants organic wine.' I knew that wasn't true. Almost every day I had visitors who said, 'We want organic wine, but we can't find it on the shelves.' I also knew that no one wanted cancer and if they hadn't made the connection between systemic pesticides and cancer yet, then they were walking around with their eyes closed. I should have put together a counter-presentation to set them right, but I had the impression their views were fixed, and I had no time to waste.

Via a *courtier* we found a *negociant* - a wine merchant – who offered us a better price than the producers' group and promised collection before harvest thus freeing up important tank space. In the French system the *courtier* often acts as go between. It's a throwback to when many Bordeaux estates were owned by nobility, and the nobles didn't want to talk directly to merchants or tradespeople. Now perhaps it's the other way around, the pointy shoed *negociants* don't want to dirty their feet on a farm. Many argue that *courtiers* are an important cog in the wheels of Bordeaux wine trade, that they have local knowledge and contacts that are important in a very fragmented wine market. The sale would give us a cash-flow injection but even at the higher price we had sold at a loss. That was the devastating reality of the bulk market. Meanwhile the producers' group that was selling organic wine they didn't communicate was organic, surprisingly sold no organic wine and dissolved.

I had completed the details for the bulk sale with the *courtier* and was feeling depressed about the loss-making price, when a smart four-by-four with French plates parked outside the tasting room. A slim young man stepped out. I met him on the terrace, and we introduced ourselves.

'I read your book *Grape Expectations*. I couldn't put it down. I had to come and visit,' he said.

'Wow. Thank you!' I replied. 'I appreciate the compliment. Thanks for buying my book.'

'I'd love to taste your wines.'

'With pleasure. Usually visits are by appointment, but I have time to do a quick visit and tasting if you like,' I said.

'That would be great,' he replied. 'A quick visit then I'll buy some wine.'

As we walked the vines it became clear he knew something about the subject. He was very interested in the biodynamic sprays that had helped us solve our downy mildew problem.

Back in the tasting room I took him through the range.

'I love your wines,' he said. 'They more than live up to my expectations after reading the book.'

We laughed at the unintended pun.

'Thank you. I'll let Sean know,' I said, hoping he would put his money where his mouth was.

'I should probably tell you I work for one of the big agrochemical companies.' He looked me in the eye for my reaction.

I felt shocked but tried not to show it. I hadn't pulled any punches against systemic chemicals on the visit of the vineyard. Was he about to announce that he would be suing me for my denouncement of the kind of products his company produced?

'I'm head of a research department. I know that what you are doing with biodynamics is the way we have to go. We have to make it easy for the big players to do what you're doing.'

'But you know biodynamics is about understanding your farm and being in it. It doesn't work by a simple recipe. It can't work as effectively working by rote with no intimate understanding of the land.'

'I know. I got that from your book. But there have to be active properties in these solutions that could replace the systemic chemicals being used today.'

'Perhaps. But then it won't be biodynamics – it will be plant-based solutions. Still very interesting,' I replied.

'It's the only way forward. The systemics will be stopped eventually and we have to have products to replace them,' he said.

He ordered ten cases. It was my biggest single end-client sale from the tasting-room door. I was stunned that I had made an impact on a key researcher in an agrochemical company. My first book was having an effect on our wine sales but also on a wider scale. His visit lifted my spirits and helped salve the loss-making *negociant* sale.

My second book, *Saving Our Skins*, launched in the UK and *Grape Expectations* was released worldwide in anglophone countries. We hosted a launch event with Martin Walker, author of the *Bruno, Chief of Police* series, and his friend Raymond, who I met at Vinexpo, as guests of honour. They were as charming as they had been in Bordeaux.

I began to receive uplifting letters from across the globe: a young woman who bought *Grape Expectations* at her local post office in a village in New Zealand; an Australian who had found it at her local bookshop; and an octogenarian who had borrowed it from his local library and then bought wine and *Saving Our Skins* direct from us. What really motivated me to keep writing and helped lift me from my perimenopausal funk were the letters that said, 'Your book made me think about the provenance of my food and wine. It changed my habits.'

I felt uplifted. Everything was flying. Our bees were doing well, we were selling books and wine. The only exception was the *negociant* still hadn't collected the bulk wine. I followed up and followed up again. The signed contract meant we couldn't sell our wine to anyone else, but it was clear that they would not collect the wine in the given time frame. It was a classic *negociant* tactic to wait until harvest when growers needed the tank space then offer a price below the market rate. At that moment cash-strapped growers would take anything if they couldn't afford more tanks since they needed somewhere to put their next vintage. I got the feeling the *negociant* was hoping to negotiate the contract down. There was no way we were doing that. Thierry regularly had us rolling with laughter at his renditions of the smartly dressed *negociant* with pointy Italian leather shoes arriving in his latest model Mercedes to squeeze another few centimes out of the farmer in his darned clothes and bashed-up van.

I had to be patient. I made myself a calming cup of lavender tea. The experience with the producer group and the *negociant* made me even more resolved to keep our focus on high-quality wine and to sell everything in the bottle rather than in bulk.

I had to sell more wine. Our savings for the trip to South Africa were almost there: we had enough for two fares, now we needed to save for another two. Mum Feely went back and forth with the chemo treatments. She had months of hellish side effects, pain, and fatigue. We thought the war was being won and began to look forward to our trip for the golden wedding anniversary the following year.

Mum's positive emails and photos of cute animals for Sophia and Ellie came through regularly and we chatted every couple of weeks. We were sure she was through the worst of it. Then her medical team did a scan to check progress and discovered that the lesions on her lung had increased significantly. The initial success of the chemo was a false message. It wasn't working despite the increased doses and horrific side effects.

I felt like I had been punched in the stomach. Mum had been so positive that she would beat the cancer and that going through hell would mean she would be well. The oncologist said there was one more treatment that could be tried but it would depend on 'the histology lump compatibility with the agent' and that would take three weeks to check. We had been given little real information about Mum's cancer and its dangers. We were in a deep fog.

CHAPTER 12

Blossom and Honey

I read more about cancer and more particularly about chemotherapy treatment. I found documentaries and some studies that seemed to show that people who had cancer and rejected chemotherapy lived longer than those who took chemotherapy. I began to realise how much of an unknown cancer was. My research into the topic also indicated that more work was being done on seeking cures to cancer, than on finding the root causes so we could stop it starting in the first place.

The hope of another treatment flickered for a moment then came back negative. Mum was relieved that she wouldn't have to go through any more terrible side effects. With no more treatments, Mum and Dad Feely began to think of plans for the future, perhaps some travel. We discussed when they might visit us again. Mum started to walk a little, to try to get her mobility back, but she was worn out. Despite having stopped the chemo the side effects continued, and she needed more medication to cope with them.

We were experiencing cancer first-hand in our family and outside the cancer epidemic was growing. A vineyard worker in the Médoc region who lost her brother to cancer started a blog called '*La bouche cousue*' – 'The sewn-up mouth'. Her brother had been the employee responsible for the sprays for a large property in the region. When she asked for the record of the molecules he had sprayed over the 20 years prior to his premature death she got no response.

She campaigned for greater awareness. In partnership with *Générations Futur*, a French association founded in 1996 to raise awareness of the dangers of pesticides, she organised the analysis of pesticide residues in the hair of workers in conventional vineyards, people living near conventional vineyards, and people 300 kilometres from where vineyards were being sprayed. The level of pesticides was highest in the vineyard workers but also very high for those living near vineyards.

We knew it. When a conventional farmer sprayed several kilometres away, I could sometimes smell it, which showed that it spread well beyond the target. Sean told me only certain sprays gave off a bad smell; many lulled you into a false sense of security with little odour. The agrochemical companies found ways to make the chemicals odourless, so we didn't suspect they were poison.

There was lack of action by political players and lack of knowledge for the majority of people. A school in the Sauternes region of Bordeaux had a level of cancer that was five times the national average. The school was surrounded by conventional vineyards. When the *Telegraph* did an article on it, they quoted a former mayor saying there was a 'law of silence' because if they stopped pesticides the local economy of Sauternes wine would collapse. They quoted the current mayor as saying: 'One cannot say there is a problem.'

The key point the article missed was that it is possible to make beautiful wine without using carcinogenic chemicals. We had been doing it for ten years and I knew a number of Sauternes winegrowers that did too. It was possible to make a living and not give people cancer.

I received an email from a couple that had read *Grape Expectations*. They were on the hunt for a house in France. Sally worked for Neal's Yard Remedies, and they were very aware of the dangers of pesticide exposure. They wanted to find a holiday house in rural France where they would eventually move. They had already visited the only 100 percent organic wine commune appellation in France but had found it too expensive. Prices there had increased significantly as it was seen by those who were aware of the dangers of pesticides as one of the few vineyard areas where it was safe to raise a family. That commune had nine winegrowers, all organic. We had around 30, of which more than half were organic.

I dreamed that one day Saussignac would be 100 percent organic. We had recently earned the official status of *territoire bio engagé*, a 'territory that is committed to organic'. It sounded good but I still ran the gauntlet with pesticide spray machines when I ran or cycled with Sophia and Ellie. While more than half of the winegrowers were organic, only about 26 percent of the farmed surface area was organic. The big players were the ones that were not organic – the ones that needed to be turned around.

Around that time a large estate in the Saussignac commune went organic and biodynamic, the conversion hot on the heels of losing a court case to a worker who had been sent to do handwork in the vineyard less than 24 hours after a pesticide spray was done. Since the exposure the worker had experienced serious nervous-system disruption: headaches and dizzy spells, so bad that they could not work or drive. The estate's owner and method of agriculture had changed. It would not turn back the damage to the health of the individual but for future employees, and for us as a commune, it was good news. There was growing awareness among farmers. Where personal experience and conviction weren't forcing the change, the financial and reputational implications of a court case, like this one, could make large businesses think twice.

France put in place a two-day course called *Certiphyto*, mandatory for all people responsible for using chemical sprays. Sean attended. At the start of the course two burly farmers were laughing like schoolboys in the back of the class, bemoaning the waste of time the course represented. They were uninterested in, and unaware of, the dangers of the poisons they routinely sprayed on their farms. By the midday break they weren't laughing. The statistics shared on the dangers of the products and the dramatic effect they were having on the wider environment had left them silent.

It was ironic that organisations spraying systemic chemicals were not allowed to send employees into the zone that had been sprayed for the required 24 or 48 hours but there was no requirement to notify walkers, clients, or schools in the area, of the no-go period. I felt more determined than ever to spread the word about why it was so important to support a healthy, no pesticide, organic agriculture. I knew the scourge of cancer was a direct result of what we were doing to the earth, and particularly what we were doing in agriculture.

As author Michael Pollan said, each of us votes for the future we want three times a day: at each meal. With every purchase we encourage the kind of production it encompasses and hence the world it represents. Organic farming delivers relatively more expensive food on the face of it, but it is the true cost as opposed to chemically farmed food where you are only seeing a part of the real cost. The pollution of the cheap chemical solutions are 'externalised' and not shown in the price – things like treating cancer and nervous-system disruption and cleaning polluted water. They are left out, set aside for someone else to pay.

Mum Feely put on a brave face when we spoke, but Dad told us she needed an oxygen machine to help her breathe at night.

'I think you should plan a trip,' I said to Sean after we hung up from the call.

'And who would look after the vineyard? You know I can't get away in the peak growing season,' he said.

It was true: no one could do the vineyard work that he did. If we missed a beat while he was away, we could lose our crop.

'I read that people with this cancer can live for years,' said Sean. 'We'll wait for our family trip next year for their golden wedding anniversary.'

In a whirlwind of visitors, summer passed, and harvest was almost upon us. We planned to hand-pick everything. I sought pickers through contacts and learned how to do the associated paperwork. Our apprentice Sandrine, who had been a significant help through the summer, was a key part of the team. She had energy and was keen to learn.

Feeling confident we could leave the vineyard with Sandrine for a few days, we booked a last-minute getaway to an ecological campsite, steps from a beach near St-Jean-de-Luz, four hours' drive away on the Atlantic coast near the Spanish border. I had confirmed a large group for the Monday long before we had the idea, so Sean and the girls left on Saturday, and I was to follow on Tuesday by train.

The day they left, Sandrine took a message down for me saying Clément from Bio Logis had called and could I call him back. I had no idea who Bio Logis was, and an internet search offered nothing.

I called the number.

'Le Vieux Logis,' said an elegant voice on the other side. 'How may I help you?'

'*Bonjour*,' I said. 'I am looking for Clément. He left a message for me to call him back.'

'Oh, Monsieur Clément,' she said. 'He's the master of the hotel.'

My heart upped its pace. Clément from Bio Logis was, in fact, the *maître d'hôtel* of our dream client Le Vieux Logis, one of the most hallowed restaurants in the Dordogne.

'Oh, thank you. That must be it. May I speak to Monsieur Clément?' I said, feeling super excited.

'I will see if I can find him.'

'*Bonjour*, Madame,' said the suave voice of Monsieur Clément a few minutes later.

'Bonjour, Monsieur Clément. It's Caro Feely from Château Feely. I think you left a message yesterday asking for me to call you back.'

'Oh yes, Madame Feely. I would like to visit to try your wines. A wine critic visited us this week and said that of the wines he discovered in Bergerac yours were some of the best. He said I had to come and taste your wines.'

'Thank you. I didn't know we had had a visit from a wine critic,' I said.

'He stopped incognito. Anyway, it's my day off on Monday so I was thinking of coming to see you.'

We agreed a time and I hung up then danced round the room punching my fists into the air.

On Monday Mr Clément visited as promised and bought several cases of two wines for his Michelin-star restaurant. Alone that night I raised a glass in celebration. Clients were coming to us without us having to 'sell'. Sean's hard graft in the vineyard was bearing fruit. A few weeks before, a Dutch importer had emailed to ask if he could import our wines. He paid for a box of samples to be shipped to him and ordered ten boxes, then twenty.

The next day I trained down to join my family near St-Jean-de-Luz. I found deep joy being with Sophia, Ellie and Sean, reading on the beach, swimming, walking. I escaped for three days, and it was bliss. Having an apprentice was making a difference. I felt grateful for the advice from my friend Francine Klur to look into it.

On our return it was a headlong rush into harvest and back to school for Sophia and Ellie. I booked the harvest team. It would be our first fully hand-picked vintage and we were excited but nervous. It was a different way of doing things. We didn't know how long it would take, particularly on the vineyards we had never picked by hand. We also didn't know what pace to expect from paid pickers as all our hand-picking to date had been done with friends and clients.

Sean was drawing out each vineyard and its quantity estimate so we could make a guess at timing, and I was preparing dinner, when Ian, Sean's brother who lived near his mum and dad, rang. He never called so I knew something was up. I handed the phone to Sean.

As they spoke Sean face clouded over. Ian said Mum Feely was not doing well; that Sean needed to come and see her. It felt like days since we had chatted with her. With the chaos of our tourist season and our escape to the beach, we had missed the signals.

The following day Sean went through the motions of his work like he was in a trance. He was in shock from the news and not sure what to do. Going from rural France to rural South Africa was a twenty-four-hour journey. Our harvest was ready, and we couldn't harvest without him. If he did go, he would get there and have to come straight back. He checked flights. His mum wasn't getting better – it sounded like she wouldn't hang on until their golden wedding or even until after harvest – but it seemed crazy to go for a single day.

Bruce, Sean's sister's husband, called.

'It's really important that you go and see your mum even if it's only for twenty-four hours. It's not how long that matters. It's the fact of being there.'

His advice helped clear our harvest-pressure-addled brains. Sean found a flight leaving the following day, Friday, and returning on Monday. While he packed his case, I called our picking team to delay the start by a day. I felt like organising the harvest was wrong, like we shouldn't be doing it, like we should be focused on our family, that Sean should be going for longer, that we should all be going – but nature would not wait for us.

Sean joined his siblings and dad at his mum's bedside, cherishing the brief moments with her and them. He crossed the world, changed seasons and continents, and returned in three days.

'Her eyes flickered recognition when I showed her the fresh figs I had packed for her but she couldn't eat them,' said Sean. 'She's on liquid food and a drip now.'

His mum loved figs and she knew our tree. We started harvest with heavy hearts.

Mum Feely passed on two days later. Even though we knew it was coming, tears poured out of me. I recalled shared moments, especially their visit over our first harvest. We raised a toast that night and wished her well on her way. I passed the tissues around the table. I loved the Irish wake idea; that everyone gets together to celebrate your life when you pass on. That's what I want when I go to the next place, a big party to celebrate and share memories. Sean was missing that. He was missing being with his family at this critical time of grieving and celebrating Mum Feely's life.

Sean focused on harvest with quiet determination. He went through the motions, but he was in shock. Missing his mum's funeral and the shared time with his family made it difficult to close the circle. Sean's sister Glynis stayed on for a few weeks with their dad then he was alone. The shock of Mum Feely's passing after almost 50 years together, hit him hard.

Sean had a constant upset stomach. Eventually he agreed to go and see our doctor, who said it was because Sean hadn't had time to grieve, to assimilate the passing of his mum. Our taskmaster, the vineyard, and its associated business did not let up – there was no getting away, no escaping. Sean needed to go back and see his dad, as much for himself as for Dad Feely. He booked a two-week trip for November when the main winemaking activity would be complete.

Hand-harvesting was different to machine-harvesting. It was convivial and slow. We started at dawn and slowly proceeded across the vineyards. It was better for us and for the grapes, the human scale and pace of it was peaceful and joyful. It gave us time to share confidences and confessions. Whereas machine-harvesting our whites had taken one short morning, now it took five mornings for a team of six. The grapes were handled gently rather than thrashed. It was hard work, but it was worth it: the grapes arrived at the winery sorted, whole, and perfect.

I noticed that Sandrine was slower than the rest. She kept standing up to stretch her back. Slim and young, she should have been one of the swiftest of the group. I asked if she was all right and she said yes. Sean noticed too. We decided I needed to have a chat with her when she returned from the next few weeks at school.

Between harvesting our whites and reds, Sean, Sophia, and Ellie harvested honey from the beehives and processed it for the first time. I returned home from a day of touring in St-Émilion and found them deep in sweetness. My feet stuck to a floor decorated with a mass of sticky spots and the fragrance of honey and beeswax engulfed me. They used a stainless steel centrifuge to separate the honey from the wax and were starting the next step of pouring the honey into glass jars. The thick liquid squeezed out in a lazy river of gold, catching reflections of the setting sun. Sean, Sophia, and Ellie formed a perfect team. I wanted to stay but I had pre-booked visitors that had arrived for a one-hour visit.

It was almost dark when I returned. Boxes of honey jars were stacked on the bench. All the stainless steel trays and pans we owned were coated in golden honey and dispersed around the kitchen. The floor hadn't escaped either; instead of spots it was an almost continuous layer of stickiness.

'Get out and leave me to clean up this mess,' said Sean. 'Take these and lick them. Out, out!'

Sophia, Ellie and I took slices of bread from our bread tin and scurried out. We scraped honey in slow waves. The aroma was rich and deep like an intense field of wildflowers but more concentrated. It was the best honey I ever tasted. We swished and lavished honey on to bread and ourselves. I felt like I was taking a honey bath. By the end there was honey everywhere, even in our hair. We licked our fingers, our lips and finally the pans themselves. By the time we had finished, the pans almost didn't need to be washed.

Sean had read that the best way to clean the honey racks and any other honey utensils was to put them outside the hive. He did this and the bees took every last sticky drop. The harvest of blossom-rich honey was especially poignant; Sean's mum's nickname was Blossom.

CHAPTER 13

Growing Pains

S ean left to see his dad in South Africa. With him away I
was engrossed in keeping the business afloat and being
a single mum. Before we knew it, Sean was back, looking
more at peace for having made the trip.

The Friday evening before Sandrine's return from two
weeks at school, she called to tell us she was pregnant and
would be on maternity leave from May to September, our
busiest time. She assured me she would continue with us
after her maternity leave. I congratulated her and thanked
her for letting us know but inside I was worried about how
we would cope with the season. I could see more falls and
a nervous breakdown in my future.

I recalled a friend in Dublin, who owned a small
business, saying he only hired men because they didn't
go on maternity leave. I was furious at his chauvinism
back then, now I could see his perspective. A third of our
manpower would be gone, and at the most critical time. I

ran to find Sean. He was pruning in the Hillside Sauvignon Blanc. He looked up in surprise.

'The mystery of the slowdown since September is solved. Sandrine is pregnant. She's tired and no wonder,' I said.

'Feck,' said Sean. 'I mean I'm pleased for her if it's what she wants, but it's not great for us.'

'She'll be on maternity leave for the whole summer and for harvest time.'

'Double feck,' said Sean. 'We should have seen it coming.'

'Yes, the signs were there.'

'It's not as if we haven't had our minds on other things,' said Sean. 'No wonder we didn't cop on.'

I thought of Mum Feely and felt tears running down my face.

'Have you looked up what happens with maternity leave? Do we have to keep paying the full salary?' asked Sean.

'I had a quick look, but it confused me,' I said. 'I'll have to call the accountant on Monday.'

That night the sheets wrapped round me in a sleepless dance. On Monday I called our accountant.

'Don't worry, the state will pay the apprentice salary while she is on maternity leave,' he said.

Sweet relief. I would have to put in the training again, but I needed someone, there was no way around it. I reminded myself of my sister Foo's words: 'challenge is opportunity'. What we were experiencing was necessary to our future; it was making way for something better.

Christmas was a couple of days away. We buried ourselves in preparations. We would be having Christmas as our family of four. Sean's brother Neal and his family had changed their plans to be with us, to go to South Africa to be with Sean's dad instead. We went to Bordeaux for the day before Christmas Eve. It felt great to be together doing something completely different to our everyday activities.

Compared to our first visit 15 years before on a holiday from Ireland, Bordeaux city was transformed. Quiet silver trams slid on green carpets – mostly living grass – through organised clean streets. A core of the central part of the city had been pedestrianised and was bliss to walk around. From the tram stop at the Place de la Bourse we walked up to the Grand Théâtre, whose restaurant *Le Quatrième Mur* was the new stomping ground for *Top Chef* judge and '*Meilleur Ouvrier de France*' - 'Best Craftsman in France' - Philippe Etchebest, directly opposite Le Grand Hôtel, where Gordon Ramsay held sway.

St Catherine Street stretched from there into the distance, the longest shopping street in Europe. We walked its entirety, Sophia and Ellie in heaven. At the largest bookshop in South-West France, *Librairie Mollat*, we discovered copies of *Grape Expectations* and *Saving Our Skins* next to the full set of *Harry Potter* books. I felt like I had arrived.

We found an organic restaurant down a side street in the old town and ordered delicious fresh salad and quiche. Like the holiday on the coast, it was luxury to have a day off. But our apprentice dilemma nagged in the back of my mind. That night we tucked the girls into bed then Sean and I finished tidying up.

'I can't take the uncertainty of this apprentice thing,' I said. 'We have to find a solution. I think we have to take a second apprentice.'

'But the same thing could happen.'

'I will only hire men,' I said.

Sean guffawed, remembering my outburst to our friend years before.

'A French *man* cleaning *gîtes*, setting tables, serving lunches? I don't think so,' he said.

'You're right, it's a long shot,' I said, biting my lower lip.

France was chauvinist, decades behind the UK and Ireland, and even further behind places like Canada and New Zealand.

'But even if you find the right person can we afford two?' Sean asked.

'We'll be financially stretched,' I said. 'But I don't think Sandrine will come back.'

'But we won't know until the end of her maternity leave after the summer,' said Sean.

'We have to take the risk,' I said.

'I'm not sure,' said Sean. 'I think you should look into finding someone just for the summer. Maybe search for both and see which candidates are best.'

With that decided, we enjoyed our quiet Christmas *en famille*. Friends Pierre and Laurence de St Viance and Thierry and Isabelle Daulhiac joined us for New Year. We usually had New Year with Pierre and Laurence in the great hall of Château Saussignac but that year I announced that the party was *chez nous*; a fancy-dress party with the themes of the colour pink and pointy shoes. Sean had a tradition of ragging Thierry about his pink sweaters and Pierre about his pointy shoes. Pierre generated hearty laughter attired in bright-pink pointy shoes, pink cape and pink underpants, his solid frame and receding ginger hair perfectly offset by his rose-coloured Superman outfit.

After the break I put a job specification on the internet, contacted schools specialising in wine tourism and started the process of sorting through résumés again. It was time to move on. I had to have help. A visit from a Master of Wine (MW) served to confirm it. He also reminded me how useless I was at getting photos with famous people I met and that visited us.

A couple of years before, I was waiting for a friend in Bordeaux airport when the automatic glass doors of the arrivals hall opened and a slight man, with greying brown hair and spectacles, clad in a tweed jacket, stepped out and stopped in the sensor zone, suspending them open.

He announced in English-accented French, 'Can someone lend me a portable phone? Mine is in my suitcase in the hold and I need to get in touch with someone urgently.'

He didn't dare step out for fear of being shut out and not being able to get back for his luggage but he was desperate for a phone.

I came forward.

'Thank you!' he said, exuding relief. 'Our flight was so delayed. I should already be at an event.'

As he talked I realised he looked familiar. By the time he finished I thought I had it.

'Are you Steven Spurrier?' I asked.

'Yes, as a matter of fact I am.'

In front of me was one of the most famous wine journalists in world. He was a columnist for *Decanter* magazine, *the* wine magazine in the UK, and second only to Jancis Robinson in renown. Steven was a household name in wine circles across the globe, perhaps even more so since the screening of *Bottle Shock*, a film about a wine competition he organised in Paris in the seventies when he owned a wine shop and school there. The despair of some of the scenes in the movie captured the angst of being a winemaker so perfectly. It was truly artful. We knew those feelings well.

'I'm here as guest speaker for a wine dinner,' said Steven. 'Thanks to you at least they know I'm on my way. May I ask who you are?'

'Caro Feely. *Enchanté*,' I said, using the French term but holding out my hand to shake his in the English way, rather than leaning over to give him a kiss on each cheek. 'We're organic winegrowers in Saussignac.'

'Oh, very interesting. I visit friends near there fairly regularly. Do you have a card? I'll come and visit you next time I'm in the area.'

I dug into my bag and handed over a business card.

'It's been a pleasure to meet you. Thank you for lending me your phone,' he said and disappeared behind the glass doors with a wave.

I was enveloped by a warm feeling of unexpected good fortune.

Since then Steven had fulfilled his promise and visited us at the farm and I had seen him at Vinexpo.

'You will have no trouble selling these,' he said on tasting our wines.

His prediction was turning out to be true. We were turning wine buyers away instead of chasing them. I regretted not taking a photo with him in the tasting room. I had missed the opportunity with two famous Irish personalities: Joe Duffy and Tony Connolly, that visited. Our wall of fame could have been growing and with it our social media following. Taking photos had not entered my head.

Anne Twist, mum of Harry Styles of One Direction, visited incognito. She enjoyed a cheese platter with friends that were regular visitors. At the time I wouldn't have recognised Harry, or his mum, so I was blissfully oblivious. Anne posted a photo of a glass of wine, the Feely tasting-room deck and vines on Instagram. A friend of ours, who was a Harry fan, spotted it. By the time I looked, the photo already had 470,000 likes but alas, no Feely branding. My daughters berated me for not recognising fame when it slapped me in the face and I berated myself for another lost photo opportunity.

Soon after, Martin Moran MW, visited en route to a Master of Wine bash in Bordeaux. It was a while since we had seen him.

'God, I can't believe how much this place has changed. You have been working hard,' he said.

'The buildings have changed, the tasting room and The Wine Lodge are new since your visit, but the biggest fundamental change is the vineyard,' I said. 'Perhaps it's harder to see on the face of it but every year we see an improvement, a change in the health of the farm. Claude Bourguignon, a top soil scientist in France, reckons if land has been farmed chemically for thirty years it will take thirty years to get full health back.'

'That will take some stamina,' responded Martin drily.

'Indeed,' I replied, picturing us in twenty years. 'But already after three years of organic conversion we saw a big difference: the chemical residues were gone; the wild orchids came back. Every year the disease resistance of the vines increases; more natural clover and other beneficial plants self-seed; biodiversity increases.'

I pointed to the clover thick around our feet as we made our way back up from the vineyard.

In the tasting room I placed two glasses and a spittoon on the table and we tasted through the range.

'Your wines have changed too. They're good – I mean, really good,' said Martin.

He wasn't one to mince his words or to give unearned compliments.

I poured the last wine.

'I think it's worth getting a Riedel glass for these reds if you have one,' said Martin. 'I sense another layer that isn't coming through.'

Riedel is a brand of crystal wine glass and it's considered one of the best because of the quality of their glass and their varietal-specific shapes. I found our two Riedel glasses that were kept for special occasions and poured the pure Cabernet Sauvignon, a new *cuvée* recently christened *Vérité*. We launched a competition for our newsletter subscribers to come up with a new name for it given certain conditions. Two people suggested *Vérité*, the name we chose from all the suggestions, so both won a signed copy of *Saving Our Skins*.

We compared the two different glasses of the same wine.

'Incredible,' I said.

'I was at a Riedel tasting a couple of weeks ago and it reminded me just how much difference it can make. *This* is the *Vérité*,' he said, holding up the Riedel glass.

We laughed.

'Wow,' I said, shaking my head in disbelief. 'It has far more fruit. The barrel aromas are still there but they're playing a support role rather than being in front like they are in the other glass. The Latin saying is '*In vino veritas*', but we could also say '*In Riedel Veritas*' for the taste of the wine.'

We tried the other reds in the Riedels. There was a difference but not as dramatic as with Feely *Vérité*.

We finished tasting and took our glasses inside to delight in Sean's duck breast in a red wine reduction sauce with homegrown potatoes and spinach paired with no-sulphite-added Feely *Grâce*. It was the perfect match; a dense, rich, mineral blend. Chat about Ireland and wine sparked. We proceeded to a selection of organic cheeses, revelling in Valérie's *tarin*, my friend from the Bergerac market who had so patiently explained why choosing organic dairy was important.

'I know it's a weekday for you, so I won't keep you up,' said Martin. 'I might take a glass of that *Vérité* with me – I have some writing to do and it will be a good companion. Thanks for a great dinner.'

I filled his Riedel glass and he set off to write in the Wine Lodge.

The following morning, I knocked on the door with the offer of coffee and muesli in our kitchen.

'Sorry to hurry you, Martin, but I need to turn the room around before the tour guests arrive,' I said after settling him in with a strong brew.

'No problem. I'll be fine here now I have coffee and Wi-Fi.'

I tore across to the Lodge, removed the sheets, raced round to put them on to wash, then returned with fresh sheets, vacuum and cleaning equipment. As I finished making the bed, Martin returned to fetch his suitcase.

'Ready to go?' I said.

'Another hard day of wine-tasting ahead of me,' he said and laughed. 'By God, you work hard. Another role you have to play: chambermaid.'

I laughed. 'Yep! I have to get this ready for clients this afternoon and I have wine-school guests arriving at ten.'

'No problem at all. It was fantastic to see you again and to see the progress you've made. You can be proud of yourselves. I know it isn't easy. Look at my friend Charles. He worked hard, made great wine and still had to sell up.'

Charles had one of the iconic estates in the region. Looking at the backdrop of him and others that had closed their doors reminded me how fortunate we were to be thriving as a small farm business.

We said our goodbyes and I raced on with the rest of my day. A few weeks later Martin covered no-sulphites-added Feely *Grâce* as his wine of the week and wrote about how we were back on '*terroir firma*' and had turned our farm around. As I read the article, I slapped my thigh realising I had missed another photo opportunity. Martin was a celebrity wine journalist regularly featured on the radio and in print in Ireland. But I could forgive myself given my workload. Sandrine had left on maternity leave, and I still hadn't found a replacement.

I waded through countless CVs and interviewed four candidates in person. None of them fit what we were looking for. Spring had arrived, the pace was gathering, and I felt like an Olympic sprinter limbering up for the spurt required to get through the six months of manic that was our season. I didn't want it to include falls, memory lapses or fourteen-hour days every day. It wasn't good for me or my family. We had to find someone – and soon.

Sean came up with wild leeks, purslane, and kale, from the garden. He took off his boots, washed his hands and started chopping. We had passed each other that morning but still hadn't actually greeted each other.

'I've been looking through more CVs. I still haven't found anyone,' I said, diving into a work discussion. 'I don't want to settle for someone who isn't passionate about organic and about wine.'

'You made that mistake the first time,' said Sean.

'Exactly,' I replied.

I didn't need reminding.

'This time we need the right person, or we'll cost ourselves more time, money and angst than if we have no one,' I said.

'But you have to have someone. You can't cope on your own,' said Sean definitively, sensing that I was preparing to lay down arms and surrender.

Our local organic association, AgroBio Périgord, suggested listing our job description on two agricultural job networks, and a promising email arrived a few weeks later. The applicant looked like our dream come true: a landscape engineer interested in all things ecological. Cécile had worked as a volunteer and *au pair* in Ireland and loved the place. She was a part-time beekeeper planning to sign up for a one-year *alternance* work-and-study wine tourism degree at a school about one hour from us in Bordeaux. I interviewed her online then organised for Sean and I to chat with her again. She was available from June, when we needed her, and could be with us for two summers plus some of the time in between during her year of school.

I sipped sage-leaf tea and reflected on our interviews. Cécile appeared dynamic and steeped in our ethos. Her CV showed useful work experience and strong organisational ability. She looked like a good fit, someone who could make a difference to our business at this critical moment in our evolution and in the process help bring a little more balance to our lives.

CHAPTER 14

Orange Wine and a New Era

My admin folder was filled with paperwork about how apprenticeship worked, the cost formulas and details like the obligatory doctor's visit required for new hires. With Sandrine the obligatory doctor's visit had created chaos. Her school said they would organise the visit for all the students. Then, because the social services organisations were split by county, so there were different doctors depending on where the employer was based, they decided not to. Only, the school didn't tell us, the employers, that the plan had changed.

A few months into the contract and shortly before Sandrine's maternity news, our accountant called in a panic to say we were being billed full-time worker social charges because the apprentice contract had not been registered since the doctor's visit had not taken place. The

MSA - the social security service for farmers - invoice for thousands of euros arrived to reinforce the message and I heard Chris' voice in my head, telling me to take ten deep breaths.

I tried calling the MSA and got no answer. They were shut during the hours I was not in front of clients, and for one full day every week, their phone lines were closed. A farmer friend had had all his bank accounts frozen for a late payment. I wasn't going to pay a bill that was incorrect, but I didn't want our accounts frozen. My frustration was at fever pitch when Sean and I visited Vinitech, a machinery and technical show for winegrowers, to investigate alternatives to our heat exchanger in the winery. I discovered one of the head honchos of MSA at the MSA stand and poured my fear and exasperation out to him. Within days I had a doctor's appointment, and the crisis was over.

For Cécile I was ready. The doctor's visit would be organised well in advance no matter what the school said. Fortunately, I had the contact details from the previous visit since the information was nowhere to be found online. We had time. Cécile arrived for a trial month, an opportunity to see if she got on with us, and to finalise the administrative aspects of her contract with us and her school.

Cécile was eager to learn and had a great sense of humour. I felt a weight lifting off my shoulders. She picked sprigs of vines and placed them in a decanter in the tasting room, bringing a touch of nature and elegance. She began working on our wine list, aiming to present it in a more pleasing and easy-to-understand format.

'What do you think of this shit?' she said.

I looked up eyes wide, not expecting her to use that language, and we both cracked up. With her French accent 'sheet' came out sounding just like, well, 'shit'.

'What do you think of this sheeeet?' she asked, after regaining her composure.

From then on when we spoke about sheets – whether a sheet for the beds in the accommodation or a sheet of paper – she would carefully stretch the word out and both of us would have a good laugh. She was a joy to be with.

Cécile's course director arrived to finalise the *alternance* contract. All was going well until we discussed the statutory rate of pay. Cécile had already been on an *alternance* contract, so she didn't fit the costing scenario I had on file. Given that Cécile had already been on a contract like this, her contract had to be set at almost 50 percent more than I had estimated. We still didn't know if Sandrine would come back. With her and Cécile on the payroll we would be in too deep and even deeper with this new higher wage. In three short weeks I had become attached to Cécile.

'I'll have to talk to Sean. It's a significant difference. I'm sure we can come up with a solution,' I said, not feeling as sure as I sounded.

That evening Sean and I talked through the new hurdle.

'How come you didn't know before?' asked Sean. 'How did you get this far without realising?'

'I had no idea there was a special clause for someone who had already done an *alternance* contract. It wasn't in the costing scenario I had from the school.'

'Well, another lesson learned the hard way,' said Sean.

'Cécile is amazing. But can we afford it? We have hefty loans in progress. We're going to take the hit of low yields from the bad flowering. Cécile will definitely bring us more business, especially in the season when we know we lose sales if I'm not here.'

'Exactly,' said Sean.

'Cécile is already making a real contribution. She's part of the team. I feel like we're working together for a common purpose. Before I think of something that needs attention she's on to it. She's been working on marketing brochures for the business and has already captured the essence of what we are better than I have in ten years. She's a dynamo.'

'She's proactive,' said Sean.

'Yes. We have to find a way to pay her,' I said, almost thinking out loud.

'There you go,' said Sean.

'Not only that, the *alternance* contracts are usually half of the term time at school and with her school it's about a third.'

'So you do know what to do,' said Sean.

I realised he had been acting like my business consultant. He had made me work out what I already knew but hadn't articulated.

With the budget discussion concluded we moved on to the naming and blending decisions for our upcoming bottling. We were in the thick of our annual reflection, a time when we spent hours trying different blends. My notebook became a spider's web of notes on different wines, barrel samples, and potential combinations. Sean poured a wine into my glass.

'Look at that colour,' he said.

It was bright orange, a most beautiful but unusual tint for a dry white wine.

'I love it,' I said after tasting it. 'What is it?'

'It's our first no-sulphite-added white wine. It's Semillon that's been in barrels for more than a year and it's so stable I'm happy to bottle it without sulphites,' replied Sean.

Sulphites are added as a preservative during winemaking to protect wine from oxidation and to stop things like re-fermentation and the development of bacteria.

I lifted the glass to my nose.

'It smells so good. Honeysuckle, oranges, *tarte Tatin*.'

'Honeycomb. A hint of quince,' said Sean.

'A touch of ginger.'

I took another sip. It was dry but it tasted like honey, flower nectar, and oranges with a hint of mineral smoke. It was unlike any white wine Sean had made – in fact, it was unlike any white wine I had experienced.

'Delicious and original,' I said. 'But will our clients accept it? It's so different.'

'I don't think we can sell it to professionals for resale unless they specialise in natural wine, like Yanflorijn Wijn in Amsterdam. You'll have to explain it on the website and make sure that people understand what it is when they're here in the tasting room.'

'What are we going to call it?'

'Honeycomb? Blossom? *Fleur de* something?' said Sean.

'What about *Mille Fleurs* or *Champ des Fleurs*?' I said.

'*Mille Fleurs* has a good ring to it,' said Sean.

I saw tears in Sean's eyes. Both of us were thinking of his mum and her nickname Blossom. This first no-sulphite white would be a homage to her.

'That's decided then. *Mille Fleurs*,' I said.

No-sulphite-added wines had become a key part of our range. We had progressed from fear of them to confidence. The first time we tried doing no sulphite-added wine it went wrong and the volatile acidity – a sign that the wine was starting its journey to vinegar – went up dramatically. We added sulphites and stabilised it, but it wasn't a wine we were going to sell under our brand. Fortunately, it wasn't a significant volume, and it was still within the appellation norms, so we sold it as bulk wine to a *negociant* who blended it with scores of other wines and sold it to supermarkets. We learned that natural wine, with no additives at all, was not for the faint-hearted. We trod cautiously after that false start.

The following year Sean's no-sulphite-added red was magnificent, my favourite red of all the wines we had made. We preferred to drink wine with low and no sulphites so it was logical that we were making our wines this way. Sulphites cause inflammation so it's better if wines contain lower levels. Organic wine guarantees lower sulphites than conventional wine and biodynamic wine even less. With *Mille Fleurs* and our other no-sulphite-added wines we were moving into a category called 'natural wine'.

Sean's confidence with no-sulphite-added wine had grown, as had the resistance of our wine to oxidation. With natural farming the level of antioxidants like resveratrol grew. The level of natural acidity was also higher and that helped to protect the wine. In addition, with hand-picking, the fruit stayed whole until it was in the winery and protected by inert gas, further reducing the need for sulphites.

We had increased to three no-sulphite-added natural wines in the range: wines made with grapes and nothing but grapes. For the rest of the range, we were certified organic and biodynamic: our wines were made with grapes and low sulphites at bottling but no other 'ingredients', unlike most industrial wine. We were making wine that would have satisfied Columella, the Roman who wrote the most important agricultural works of his time, and said 'we consider the best wine is one that can be aged without any preservative; nothing must be mixed with it which might obscure its natural taste.'

We moved on to the red samples. I lifted the *Résonance* Merlot to my nose.

'Hmm. Dark fruit, a hint of truffle. The deep cool of the limestone.'

'Plum and blackberry,' said Sean.

'It's incredible that this is from the same vineyard as our first few years of *Résonance*. It's yummy,' I said.

I had never been able to say 'yummy' about our Merlot from the north facing Garrigue block before. It was from my least favourite red vineyard but now it was surprising me. I could see a net progression over the years that proved the wisdom of going organic and biodynamic. Our yields were low but our quality went up every year. It was a long game.

'What's the sulphite level?' I asked.

'It will be around sixty milligrams per litre at bottling. It's low, not "no". The next vintage of *Résonance* is no sulphite added, but I'm not sure we should risk going no sulphite on all of it. We'll see when the time comes to bottle it next year. I didn't bring a sample but it's even better than this one.'

Sean was not one to sing his own praises, so it had to be good.

'The next few barrel samples are no sulphite added,' said Sean. 'This one is hand-picked Merlot from Hillside vineyard.'

'Very smooth,' I said after sniffing, taking a sip and spitting. 'Lovely notes of dark and red fruit: plum, cherry, raspberry. A hint of chocolate.'

I wrote furiously, trying to capture our perceptions of the different wines. Sean did what the French call *aviner*: pour a little of the next wine into the glass and throw it out. This rinsing of the glass with the same wine ensures a more accurate reading of the sample.

'This one is thick with *cassis*, dark cocoa and bitter orange. It's lovely and smooth,' I said.

'It's the hand-picked Cabernet Sauvignon, also no sulphite. Let's try those two together in the proportions we have.'

He poured into a beaker then into my outstretched glass.

'That tastes like it should be *Grâce*. Delicious. I love it. These wines are so good, Sean. There's depth of flavour and harmony like a symphony.'

'But I'm not sure I want to do the heavy work of the winemaking anymore,' he said.

'What?' I said, then sat in stunned silence for a second. The wines were finally showing the potential of our hill farm and Sean was saying he didn't want to do it. 'But you're so good at it – these wines are magnificent.'

'I like growing the grapes, I love gardening, but I don't like doing the pipe and barrel work in the winery,' said Sean.

'Shoot, Sean,' I said, although I couldn't blame him. Our winery was far from automated. I wouldn't want to do it. 'What will we do?'

'Maybe we can get someone to do the winemaking.'

'But what would you do for work at that time of year?' I asked.

'Go travelling.'

I laughed heartily. 'If we were in California or Australia, perhaps it would be easy to get a contract winemaker. But these wines are great because you made them. It isn't just the vineyard and the growing. You don't realise how much experience you've built up in this kind of winemaking.'

'I know.'

'Perhaps we *could* get someone to take over for a few months and go travelling. It would do both of us good.'

As tempting as the thought was, I knew it was a long shot. I put it aside and tried to concentrate on the rest of the samples. Bottling was weeks away and we needed to finalise the blends.

We bottled the new wines, including the no-sulphite-added *Mille Fleurs* white and the *Grâce* and *La Source* reds. I confirmed with Cécile and her school that we wanted to go ahead with the contract. We would find a way to meet the commitment.

Soon after, Cécile and I attended Expressions Bio at Vinexpo with our freshly bottled range of natural wines. It was great to be there, but my friends Clément and Francine Klur were not attending, and I missed them. We had a good position on a corner stand. Our only neighbour was from a large inherited family estate and he had 'people' doing all the work for him. He lived in the city and visited his estate once a week. He was an absentee farmer. I missed the Klurs even more.

Steven Spurrier, the world-famous wine journalist I had met in the airport, and star of the story in the film *Bottleshock*, visited our stand. Cécile dived into the wine sessions that were available as part of the show and attended a session on Georgian wines offered by Steven.

'Caro, he was so good. Compared to the other presenters he was amazing.' She was impressed by him, but also excited that such a wine guru had made time to visit our stand. As we packed up, I realised I had missed yet another photo opportunity.

We caught a lift back to Saussignac with Gaby and Julien Cuisset, two young locals in the process of taking over the family vineyard business. Cécile made friends easily and by the end of the trip was exchanging contact details with them. In a few short weeks Cécile had become part of the farm, part of the team, part of Saussignac.

⇢⇢⇉ ⇇⇇⇇

Late spring temperatures hit 35 degrees. It was the hottest month of what turned out to be the hottest year on record. On a day that was designated 'fruit' on our biodynamic calendar, our fig tree was radiating such a strong aroma of fig that I felt like lying down in its shade and drinking in the scent, but I needed to get to school to collect Ellie.

Near the school gate I stood under a fig tree growing on Natalie's fence line. Natalie had been Ellie and Sophia's teacher and she lived across the road from the school. I loved knowing these good people around me; there was a sense of security in it. I sniffed a leaf hanging close and was transported into the fig's cool, deep world. The tree had positioned itself next to Natalie's old well, roots deep in limestone and a water source. The fruits were still hard and scent-free, but the leaves respired rich fig notes.

At home Ellie and I picked cherries in the heat of the evening, swaying in the tree like sloths – one for the basket, one for me. Filled with cherries, I walked Dora to the bottom of Garrigue Merlot. The sunset across the hills to the west was a profusion of golden glory. Grasses and wheat ears undulated in the soft warm breeze between vineyards, plum orchards, and hedgerows. The hills drifted away like dunes alternating gold and green. As I passed a walnut tree I stopped and reached for a luminescent lime-green leaf. It was smooth and satiny. I inhaled above the leaf and was engulfed in the aroma of walnuts. Like the fig, its entire being was respiring, radiating its fruit aromas. I felt like I would explode with happiness, gratitude and joy for this beautiful place, for the wonders of the nature that surrounded me.

Cécile was a gem and I soon discovered we shared a passion for figs. We moved from spring to late summer in a whirl of guests. With the figs now ripe, Cécile made it her mission to pick fresh figs every day for the lunches served as part of our half or full day tours. Clients loved it and so did we.

The luscious purple fruits were plump and sweet. Each day there were some left, and I took them inside, finishing my day with a few, and then starting the next with a few more. The fig season was long that year; the ripe figs kept coming. Then Cécile discovered the green figs at the southern end of the farm. Fully ripe they were even more heavenly than the purple ones and we gorged on figs once more.

The day after the green fig feast, I woke up with my palate transformed and not in a good way. Nothing tasted right, not my tea, nor – more importantly – the wine we served in the tasting room. Given that my job involved tasting wine every day it would be a catastrophe on a professional level, not to mention on a personal one, for my eating and drinking pleasure. Food was bland, tea was horrible, and wine was worse. What had caused it? Had I done permanent damage?

The next day I visited Antoine at Cadet-Bon in St-Émilion, the winemaker who had come to my aid when I had the puncture. As we walked down to taste the grapes in his vineyard, he pointed to a fig tree filled with bounty.

'They look good but don't eat them. When I first started with Derenoncourt Consultants, I remember Stéphane saying to me, "Never eat figs when you are tasting grapes. They mess up your tasting capability."'

'Holy smokes, Antoine,' I said. 'I have had a problem with my sense of taste the last couple of days. Nothing tastes right. Wine tastes awful.'

'No way. For real?' responded Antoine, horrified at the idea.

'Yes,' I said, laughing a little crazily. 'Now I know why: too many figs! I've been eating more figs than ever; the season has been so good. I never knew they could wreck my taste buds. I'm wishing I copied Robert Parker and insured my palate for a million bucks.'

Robert Parker was the most famous wine critic in the world towards the end of the 20th century. He famously insured his palate.

'No, Caro. You mustn't worry. It should come back in a few days. But it's not ideal for a wine professional like you, so you will have to hold back on the figs.'

I didn't know which was worse, the deviated palate or giving up my favourite fruit, but I was relieved to know the cause. Cécile had a similar feeling but less pronounced. In two days, her palate was back to normal while mine was worse. I went searching on the internet for more information. Figs could attack the lining on your mouth, a bit like tannins did. The white of the skin of the fig, much more pronounced on green figs, was responsible. The effect was far worse in, and after, menopause – which was why mine had persisted and Cécile's was gone.

I thought that I had almost licked this unpleasant phase of life, that I had got the upper hand over its violent and suicidal effects, but now it hit me with a nasty sting in the tail, or rather, in the tongue. I faked it through the wine-tasting classes, talking based on what I knew about the wines but unable to taste, my mouth like sandpaper.

Just when I thought my mouth would never be the same again, my taste buds returned. I hadn't touched figs for a week. I didn't touch them for a few more days then I gingerly started again, peeling each one carefully before eating it, avoiding the green ones, and vowing to eat the rest in moderation. Menopause had had the last laugh on this figaholic.

⟶⟩⟩⟩ ⟨⟨⟨⟵

Sandrine was due back soon. I followed up with emails and phone calls over the weeks, asking about her baby and when she would be back. Eventually, a couple of days before she was supposed to be back with us, she emailed to say she would not be returning after all. We were fortunate to have Cécile on board.

Cécile was already doing half-day visits on her own, handling groups with skill. By the following summer she would have experienced a full growing cycle and be able to talk even more knowledgeably about Feely vineyard. She researched new organic food producers, slowly changing our lunch suppliers from large-scale organic producers to small local organic producers that we knew first-hand. She created a pairing 'sheeeet' to make it easier for our visitors to follow the wine and food pairing.

The ferocious heat of late spring had followed through into summer and meant an early start to harvest. We arrived back from a few days at the campsite near St-Jean-de-Luz and realised that our white grapes were ready. We swiftly booked the team. Despite harvesting ten days earlier than ever our Sauvignon Blanc juice displayed a hefty 14 degrees of potential alcohol. I worried that we had missed that elusive balance, the perfect harmony between alcohol and acidity.

'Perhaps we should have picked earlier?' I said to Sean.

'We went as fast as we could,' he replied. 'Anyway, if we had, it would have been too acidic, and we would have had green notes. Look at the lime and grapefruit character it has, and the level of acidity. We couldn't have gone any earlier. As the vintages get hotter, we'll be walking a tightrope.'

'More than we are already?' I asked, eyebrows raised.

Then it was the waiting game for the red grapes. We debated 'Will we harvest or won't we?' With each splatter of rain, I felt butterflies in my stomach. Then it poured and we questioned waiting. I visited St-Émilion with clients and Antoine said they had had no rain. I felt jealous. Perhaps we should have picked before the deluge.

On Thursday I collected clients from the station. There was so much rain that the road from Gardonne was like a river. I could barely concentrate on our guests' questions. The amount of rain pouring down could damage the grapes and make picking a nightmare.

'What will this mean for quality?' asked Mary, one of the new arrivals.

'Oh, we hope it will be OK since we're up on the hill, so the water drains away,' I said, thinking meanwhile, *we're toast*.

That evening I attended yoga with my friend Isabelle. The yoga room was spacious and peaceful. Large windows looked on to a starry sky. Sometimes I felt out of place, like an imposter, not a natural yoga practitioner. Some French words for specific body parts were not familiar to me, like *clavicule* for collarbone. I lagged behind but the teacher put me at ease saying to the group: 'It doesn't matter what the others are doing. What's important is that you feel comfortable. Listen to your body. Take your time.' It was totally unlike a city gym studio: there were no mirrors, no music. There was calm. We always ended with ten minutes of relaxation. I realised that the classes offered more than yoga movement. At the end of the session, I felt relaxed – truly relaxed – an unusual sensation in harvest time.

More rain fell. What had promised to be a good vintage was looking more and more like it could be a failure. Sean walked the vineyards again and assured me there was no problem. Between deluges I had another set of clients for the Wine Adventure Day.

'When it comes to winemaking, how we pick and when we pick are key. It's a time of great joy and community but also of great angst. Our whole year's work hangs in the balance,' I said as we started the afternoon session.

'Isn't that right,' said Karen. 'My family have a vineyard in New Zealand. We checked a parcel of Shiraz, and it was perfect. Three days later when the pickers arrived, two thirds of it were rotten. It was that fast. I couldn't believe it.'

I felt a twist of fear and struggled to focus as I presented the winemaking steps. As soon as the guests and Cécile left, I went to check the Merlot and realised that Sean was right. The grapes still looked good. My afternoon of stress had helped no one and had hurt me. I called my friend Laurence to see if she was available for a walk. I needed to find perspective. Gossiping with her about everything other than harvest would help. It did. After walking in the forest below the village, we sat in the Saussignac Castle courtyard enjoying the setting sun. Looking at the golden rays pouring onto the scene like honey, I realised how sweet life was, each precious moment a blessing.

I had created my own suffering that afternoon. I was always edgy at harvest and menopause made it worse. I needed to calm down. Back home I decided to do some brainless chores, starting with moving the packed-up boxes from the Cottage to our side of the house. The Cottage was due to undergo a renovation that winter and we were emptying it of its contents. As I carried a box of linen, I noticed the duvet cover bought decades before when Sean and I first moved in together. For ten years it had been in service in the Wine Cottage, and we had used my old down sleeping bag unzipped and thrown over darned sheets.

I pulled the cover out of the box. The cream linen with a simple embossed border looked almost new. It would be perfect for our bed. The find was a catalyst to tidy the tiny bedroom Sean and I shared. Our room had some shelf space but no hanging space. Our shoes were stacked neatly on the floor in Château Feely boxes. I cleared the surfaces then shook my old sleeping bag into the cream cover.

The gesture of taking back the cover was liberating. It felt like freedom, like I was taking a little of our life back from our all-consuming enterprise. It felt like a grand moment, a realisation. We were on the road to better balance in our lives. I put the matching pillow covers on to our pillows and then placed a cushion with lavender sprigs embroidered by Mum Feely on top. I thought of her for a moment and felt tears flowing down my cheeks. With the new covers and the cushion, our bedroom looked beautiful and cared for, like it had had a makeover.

Back in the Cottage I measured up the walls of the end room for the new kitchen and a memory washed over me. Toddler Sophia and baby Ellie propped up in the double bed, wrapped in winter clothes and blankets for a bedtime story. The four of us lived in this end room for a year as we renovated the first part of the house so we could rent it out as a self-catering unit.

Now Sophia was almost a teenager, but she behaved like a reliable adult. She would wake at 5.45 a.m. and then wake the rest of the house at their requested times. She made her own breakfast, her homework was done, her bag was packed for the day and there was never a rush. She called me when it was time to go to school, so I didn't have to watch the clock. Ellie was also top of her class or close to the top, but grumpy and slow in the mornings. They had both become fashionistas. They helped with the lunches and cleaning the accommodation to earn money for clothes.

I still wore clothes bought with one of my first pay cheques nearly 30 years before and I hadn't done much clothes shopping since we started our organic vineyard adventure. Now I hit the high street of Bergerac with my fashion-conscious daughters and found it was fun.

The following day as we walked to school, Ellie recited a poem about vines. It was beautiful, lyrical, and sensual. Dressed in new black skinny jeans, grey boots and her bright red coat, a hand-me-down from a friend, she looked so chic and grown up, like she could have walked out of a *Vogue* magazine. She took my breath away.

We picked the red grapes and my worries proved unfounded. The juice was beautiful, and the subsequent wine looked like it could be another grand *millésime*, the French word for 'vintage'. The unusual heat gave a quality to the scenery reminiscent of Chinese etchings. By November the light were like nothing we had experienced. We walked to school marvelling in the golden shafts of mist layering through the side valley between Gageac and Saussignac.

With the UN Climate Change Conference in Paris coming up, I read more about the out-of-control train coming down the track. I was struck by how little the journalists talked about what each of us could do to contribute to the solution. It was all about the big picture;

talks about what governments could do with carbon trading; massive, complex solutions. There was a lot of 'we hope to' in the final agreement and not a lot of consequence for those who didn't. The consequences would be for all of us but worse for those already living precariously, close to sea level, in semi-desert, and in storm belts. I was surprised that the talks didn't include much on how agriculture could contribute to the solution. Organic natural farming sequesters - captures and stores away - carbon dioxide, while chemical farming generates carbon dioxide and toxic nitrate gas.

My yoga sessions with Isabelle were a sacred part of my week. She offered wisdom on school in France, adolescence – her sons were a couple of years ahead of our daughters – and administrative challenges. En route we chatted non-stop; I enjoyed the time to chat with a girlfriend almost as much as the yoga. A full Sunday of yoga with a visiting teacher was proposed and we signed up. I wondered if my mind and body would be able to handle it but went ahead anyway.

CHAPTER 15

One Yogi and Five Tibetans

'In this silent moment of "now", of being fully present, we feel a great sense of peace,' said Xu Yen.

His round face radiated happiness and belied his age. Yoga was clearly doing something for his longevity, health and state of mind. He chatted warmly, initiating the session with words of wisdom.

'Enjoy every moment of life. In the depths of the ordinary moments, we find the extraordinary.'

Every few minutes his discourse lightened up and he exploded with mirth. It was so infectious I laughed, even without understanding all of what he was saying in his heavily accented French. Then, almost without us noticing, he started a sequence of yoga moves and we followed.

'You see, we are doing nothing here. Nothing,' he said.

It felt like nothing the way he presented it, but I knew it was something. He was a master yogi. As the day progressed, I realised my concerns had been misplaced; instead of not coping physically or mentally, I felt energy building within me. Even after a luxurious lunch in the tradition of *auberge espagnole*, the French saying for 'bring and share', I was energised. We feasted on a large vegetable soup made by Michèle, the founder of the *Eveil du Souffle* Yoga Association; quiches, breads, cheeses, and salads; then fruit and sweet tarts to finish. A walk around the farm lake, looking in on the dairy cows and vines of Michèle's organic farm, eased our digestion. Her twenty-year-old son joined us for part of the day. At lunch he displayed the healthy appetite of a young farmer.

'So, we will start slowly,' said Xu Yen. 'I will give your stomachs time to digest. For some of us that is more necessary than others.'

He gave Michèle's son a knowing look and then reverberated with mirth. 'Yes, I see everything. He he he.'

As the sun set, there was joy in my core, a lightness of being. We had done yoga all day, but my body had no pain and no stiffness. I was a yoga convert. I made it my mission to do a couple of yoga moves at home a few times a week in addition to my evening with Isabelle. Xu Yen's state of health and happiness was proof of what yoga could do, but it was more than that. I had less backache; I was more supple. I felt better than I had in a long time, and I was sleeping better. Yoga felt right. It felt like part of what we were about.

Another key part of what we were about was connecting with like-minded people. Sandra and Santi of Simply Permaculture and Simply Canvas joined us for soup and a sandwich the day our brother-in-law Bruce arrived for the Christmas holidays. Sandra, originally Dutch, and Santi, French Sri Lankan, had met at Plum Village, a Buddhist monastery founded by Thích Nhất Hạnh and located less than ten minutes from our farm. They followed the life of a Buddhist monk and nun for years and independently decided to return to secular life. Later they met up in Ireland, where Santi had settled, fell in love, and decided to come back to France to set up a smallholding in the same region as Plum Village. Their glamping holidays farm had recently added a permaculture garden open to visitors. We always met in winter to exchange ideas on self-sufficiency and tourism. As usual, they were bursting with new initiatives.

Bruce had arrived from Mauritius that morning. His children and Glynis, Sean's sister, would follow a few days later. We hadn't seen him in eight years. I recalled that when we met 20 years before, he had assured me that glyphosate - the most widely used chemical herbicide - was non-toxic; so lovely, in fact, that I could drink a glass of it no problem. Now Bruce had barely stepped through the door, and we were already in a heated discussion about whether organic agriculture could feed the world. I knew it could, and that the chemical option would starve the world by leaving the land unfit for agriculture after a few decades.

'Fight, fight, fight!' chanted Santi, like kids would in a playground.

We cracked up. He had defused the situation with a simple gesture.

By the time we said goodbye to Sandra and Santi, we were crackling with excitement about a permaculture vineyard, and Bruce and I had steered clear of any more heated arguments. But it was the start of the *vacances de Noël* and I wondered if we would find more 'fight fight fight' situations. He was a strict disciplinarian but deeply loyal and loving. At just over 50 he was ahead of us in age but the first out running in the morning even after a few glasses of wine the evening before.

The following morning, Bruce opened my office door and peered in as the dawn was breaking.

'Have you heard of the Five Tibetans?' he asked, his breath billowing out like plumes of smoke in the cold air.

'No, who are they?' I said.

'A set of exercises a neighbour does on the beach every morning. He swears by it. He's fifty and you wouldn't know it. I'll show you when I get back from my run.'

Bruce lived a few paces from the beach in Mauritius. For a few years his work had taken him there and he had been juggling life between his family in the UK and the island.

'I'm in – anything to get you to close that door!' I said.

We both laughed. He closed it and took off.

When he returned, we rolled out yoga mats in the tasting room and he showed me the routine. It was simple and quick, and I felt good after doing it. I needed something to make me feel good since I was in the thick of a new task that French bureaucracy had thrown at us.

'You have to join a voluntary compulsory health scheme on behalf of your employees,' explained the accountant on the phone. 'It's the new law and you must have it in place by January.'

I was a little surprised by the idea of this new scheme being both voluntary and compulsory but it was an oxymoron I had already encountered in France so I knew that questioning it would be futile.

'Do you have any suggestions of who we should sign up with?' I asked, hoping she would make it easy for me.

'We're not allowed to make recommendations. You can sign up with the company you like. Look online and I'm sure you'll find one that fits,' she replied.

I heard an advert on the radio for an international health insurance company, then received a cold call and found them online. They offered a package at half the price of the one proposed by our local bank's partner, plus they were friendly on the phone, and I could do everything online. It seemed too good to be true. After a quick search for other alternatives, I decided it was the one and signed up. Everything was smooth and super easy.

The following day I received an email inviting me to add my employees to the policy I had created. I went online with Cécile's details, hoping to get this task off my list. The time it had taken in investigation and administration was already way out of line, another victory for French bureaucracy.

I got to the second page after filling in Cécile's details down to her great-aunt's favourite pet and then it asked me for her *centre RO*, *caisse RO*, *code grand regime* and *rang de naissance*. I was stuck. I looked through the papers I had and found nothing of this order. I tried calling. All the lines were busy. I waited patiently in the queue and my call was dropped about ten minutes later. I tried again and had the same experience.

Then it was past business hours and the helpline closed. The page I had been working on closed with a session timeout. I logged in to see if it had kept the details from the first page that I had validated and found it had saved nothing. I walked outside and howled into the wild winter night.

The following day I contacted the administrator that helped us with payslips and asked if she knew what these codes were.

'*Ah mince*. You can't sign up with that company. The agricultural unions in the Dordogne have done a deal with a single company. That's the only company you can sign up with.'

Now the new voluntary compulsory scheme was also a monopoly.

'If they did that, why didn't they pass the administration directly through the MSA and charge it as part of all the other voluntary compulsory payments?'

'You could ask that,' she said.

'It's the same company that was proposed by our bank. It's almost double the price of the one that I've signed up to,' I said.

'I know,' she said.

'It seems like a commercial gift for the company,' I said.

'You could say that,' she said.

I hung up feeling beaten. French bureaucracy had me crushed; I didn't even have the energy to howl a second time.

Bruce gave me a one-page outline of the 'rites' often shortened to 'The Five Tibetans' by those in the know. Over the following days I went through them either alone or with Bruce. After three times I remembered them without needing to look at the page. Each time I did it I felt good.

I found a moment in business hours to call the company I had signed up with. After ten minutes of queuing, I explained my dilemma to the call centre representative. She said the only way to unsubscribe was to handwrite a letter to the company headquarters and rattled off the address.

Then I went to the voluntary compulsory monopoly company's website hoping that signing up with them would be as easy as with the people I had just had to un-sign from. There was no information about the product I needed, no way of getting in touch easily, no email address or direct phone number for a local agency. I filled in a contact form and waited for a response. I waited two days then sent a reminder. Still there was no response. I took ten deep breaths. I was trapped in a time-wasting loop. I could not have written a better imaginary skit on French bureaucracy than this reality. The next day I went back to the website and sent another request. I emailed my bank that had originally told me about this company's offer. I heard nothing. I had spent days researching and trying to implement something that had been decided for me but that was now proving impossible to put in place.

'How can you soar like an eagle?' I moaned out loud.

'When you're a turkey,' said Ellie, looking in the door.

'He he he,' I laughed.

My emails and calls disappeared into a black hole like my howl into the night; months later I was still waiting. Everyone knows that monopoly is not an optimal solution for efficiency or for the good of the economic participants. Now I knew it was not good for my karma either. I rolled out the yoga mat and did the Five Tibetans to bring order to my disturbed spirit.

There was something about doing these five exercises that restored balance – perhaps even hormonal balance – inside me. Perhaps I was naturally reaching the end of menopause or perhaps there was magic in them. The backache and stiffness I experienced when I spent too much time at the computer vanished; I felt energised. The swathe of grey developing in my hair even seemed to be reducing.

⌁

The outline of the leafless oak next to the winery was stark against the winter sky. I sat on the bistro chair outside the kitchen door and pulled on my wellies. Sean had finished pruning the Semillon vines so now it was over to me to remove the cut wood from the trellis. Pulling wood was therapeutic. The sounds of winter birds and the rhythmic twang of the wires mingled. Each vine was like a movement in a dance. Grab the canes, yank downwards, drop the freed wood into the middle of the row, bend to gather up the canes that dropped at the foot of the vine, throw them into the middle of the row, pull away any remaining bits. Stretch up tall. Step across to the next vine. Start the dance again.

It was like a yoga movement, a meditation, especially if the sun was out and we weren't under pressure. Bruce joined me and we worked together, chatting, sharing experiences from the years since we had seen each other. He created a motivational force to get things done. During our second French summer he and his children, Duncan and Emma, came to camp with us and we mowed down projects like they were skittles. This time was no different.

His extra manpower helped us grub up a section of ancient vines. We loved our old vines, but these ones had become too sparse in number, and in yield, to keep. Sean chain-sawed each vine near the base. Then we declared the status to the customs authorities so they could validate it before we removed the wood, the trellis system, and then the roots. There was a pre-grubbing up form and a post grubbing up form. It was red tape heaven. Pulling the wood was easy, dismantling the trellis wires and poles, a little more complicated. It was possible to rent or purchase a wire winder that worked on the tractor's power take-off (PTO) but we found horror stories of people being strangled by the contraption. Thierry Daulhiac passed by and we asked his advice.

'Oh. Yes, it can be dangerous or, he he, funny. Joel's father-in-law was helping him roll up the wire and it grabbed on to a hook on his pants and ripped them off. He was standing in the vineyard in his underpants. He he he.'

I found it strange how winegrowers talked, and even laughed, about the dangers of our *métier*, as if it were normal to risk life and limb every day as part of your job. We weren't into strangulation or losing our pants, so we decided to use our hand-operated roller, preferring a little extra work to potentially losing our lives. Over the next few days, Bruce, Sean, and I rolled up two tons of wire and stacked a mountain of old wood trellis poles that would serve to heat the house for many winters.

We took a morning off from clearing trellising and Sophia, Ellie, Bruce, and I, cycled to Gardonne for the Sunday market. We bought a chicken from a local producer and organic supplies from a newcomer to the market, a lady in a *roulotte* - a wagon - who offered dry organic products in bulk bins. Christmas carols warbled through the speakers strung around town; there was a general feeling of good cheer in the air. Stocked up with supplies, we settled down on a low wall on the square to enjoy crusty *croissants* and *pains aux raisins* and bask in the clear winter sun, taking in the chatter, colours, and aromas of the market. It was enchanting, a reminder of what we loved about rural France – the markets, the food, a slower pace of life, time to chat – things we had been missing of late in our frenetic lives.

After coercing ourselves back into our saddles we headed for home. Bruce and Sophia streaked ahead, and Ellie and I lingered a few hundred metres behind. We crossed the train track and passed a hunter walking back into the village in combat gear with his shotgun hanging over his shoulders. About 50 metres on Ellie stopped. I pulled in alongside her. She was white as a sheet and wide-eyed.

'What's wrong, *mignonne*?' I said.

'Who's that man?' she asked.

'It's just a hunter like we see every Sunday,' I replied.

'But what's he doing going into Gardonne like that?' she said, her voice shaky.

'He's probably walking home after hunting.'

'I was worried he was going to shoot the people at the market,' said Ellie.

I held my bike with one hand and hugged her tight with the other arm, trying to transfer a sense of safety. I could feel her heart racing.

'I was so scared, Mummy.'

In the past Ellie would not have had this reaction to a hunter walking on the road. It was a stark reminder of the

2015 terrorist attacks in Paris. The ripples in the psyche of her generation were perhaps greater than we had realised.

'I'm so sorry, my lovely,' I said, as I held her tight.

'I was so scared, Mummy,' she repeated.

'Oh, my lovely,' I said, holding her. We remained there in a deep embrace as cars passed and life continued around us. Her heart calmed and I released her.

'Are you OK to carry on?' I asked.

'Yes, but I feel so tired.'

'It's exhaustion after the adrenalin of being scared and getting a shock,' I said. 'We'll take it slowly.'

We took off again. Ellie stopped every couple of hundred metres to check in with me and catch her breath.

The next day Duncan, Emma and Glynis arrived, and we went pulling wood together. It was fun working and catching up on years missed. Soon we were singing and working. Duncan and Emma had beautiful voices. Duncan was part of an a cappella group at St Andrews University called *The Other Guys*, one of the top groups of their kind in the UK, with professional CDs and videos, the proceeds of which went to charity and raised awareness of St Andrews. Not that St Andrews needed help for recruitment: it was famous as a matchmaking university since Prince William met Kate Middleton there.

'You know, a couple of days ago I was at Bonny's and Jean-François, another winegrower, came in with a huge smile on his face,' said Sean. 'Mr Bonny asked why he was so happy. He said, "I have two Portuguese people pruning for me, and they are singing and working. It's two decades since I heard people singing like that in the vineyard. It brings joy to my heart." I can say the same thing.'

We were having fun and munching through the work. What would have taken me months on my own had taken a couple of days for our large family group.

That evening we wandered up to Saussignac for dinner. Glynis and Bruce walked ahead holding hands like young lovers.

'Why don't you and Papa ever hold hands like that?' asked Sophia.

I could have said, 'Because we've lost touch with each other. Because we're working too hard. Because, because...' But I didn't because I didn't know the answer. Instead, I caught up with Sean and took his rough hand in mine. It felt good. I wondered why we didn't do it.

On Christmas Day the sun was shining and a polar swim left us feeling bright and alive. As I prepared scrambled eggs, I asked Emma if she could recognise parsley and to fetch me some. She nodded and instead of heading for the garden she opened the fridge. I realised how differently we were living to the majority of the world's population. We were connected to nature, earth, and sky, every day.

As humanity we had to find a way to reconnect with nature. It would bring happiness and change the world. If we all grew some of our own food, we would store carbon through those plants and prevent the carbon dioxide emissions generated by transport required to bring food to us. Small local farms are key to this renaissance, but making a living as a small farmer is tough.

To make it work we had diversified into tours, a wine school and accommodation. The Wine Cottage accommodation renovation was almost complete. The timing had already been pushed out two months and each day took us closer to when clients were due to arrive.

Tomas, our mason, appeared at the door.

'We are short of a few tiles,' he said.

'That's strange, I ordered an extra ten percent,' I replied.

'I know but with all the cuts we have lost quite a bit.'

'OK. I'll phone the supplier to see what they can do.'

I had searched Bergerac and Sainte-Foy-la-Grande for the perfect tiles. In the end I had made a special order based on a catalogue photo, a true test of my renovation mettle. Each time I thought of it between order and arrival I felt a spike of adrenalin. When the order arrived the tiles were beautiful, exactly what I was looking for. The risk had paid off. I called the supplier.

'Ah no, that was a special order. We don't have it in stock,' he said. 'I have a single display tile that I could give you.'

'I'm not sure one will do it. We need two or three,' I said.

'Then we're really cornered. I can't put a special order in for two or three tiles. It needs to be a good volume. Anyway, even if we did order like last time, it would take at least six weeks to arrive.'

'*Mince*. Please keep the display tile for us *alors*. We'll collect it today,' I said, praying it would be enough.

Tomas collected the tile and they carefully sorted the cut pieces and made up what was missing. They finished the floor so perfectly it was complete to my eye, but for them the last section would have been better if they had had the extra tile.

I took ten deep breaths. I had learned another lesson: when doing a special order, add 15 percent. I would be 'building wise' when Château Feely was finished but 'finished' was a relative term. The four person Wine Lodge completed a few years before already needed a touch up. A living business and farm was an ongoing circle of renewal.

The Bristow family went home, leaving joy and gratitude in their wake. I had learned the Five Tibetans and with their help our farm work was well advanced, and we could look forward to our long-awaited trip to South Africa.

I had a dawn call with potential house-sitters Margherita, an Italian writer who preferred writing in English, and Nick, an Aussie photographer. They ran *The Crowded Planet*, a travel blog about their non-stop travel lives and were looking forward to touching down in France for a few weeks to catch up on months of material from exotic locations. As I flicked through their blog, I felt envious of their footloose lifestyle. Maybe I needed to look at Sean's suggestion of going travelling for part of the year more seriously. Despite the bad reception of the call from their hotel in Indonesia, the tone of their blog and the brief conversation were enough to know we had found a match. I ticked 'confirm house-sitters' off my list. It would be a first for us to leave our precious farm for longer than a week but with Cécile on-site most workdays and this responsible pair we were feeling as sure about it as we could be.

CHAPTER 16

Back to Our Roots

Our flight from Bordeaux to Paris was smooth but the line-up at Charles de Gaulle customs was a two-hundred-metre snake seething with worried or plain impatient people. There was one booth open and three international flights to process. A 'jump the queue' feeder for first- and business-class passengers ensured that the rest of us moved at a wounded snail's pace. French citizens had a special automated queue that worked intermittently.

An Asian lady raced past us, saying politely, 'I'm sorry but I'm very late. I'm going to miss my connection.'

We happily let her through – we had been there before. The airport official controlling the entrance to the queue clicked over, heels tapping officiously.

'Do the queue,' she said, her arm blocking the lady's way.

'But I will miss my flight.'

'I don't care. Do the line. I will call you.'

The woman went to the back, cowed, anxiety written all over her face and in her movements.

I felt like smacking the control freak. She clearly hadn't got the memo that an angry menopausal monster woman was passing through. Violence came naturally to me as opposed to the expected *sagesse* of ageing.

Two minutes later, the official shouted, 'Anyone for Seoul, Korea?'

The anxious lady stepped forward, relief flooding her features. I felt myself relax.

Several hours later, our Cape Town airport experience could not have been more different. All the booths were working, and the queue flew through. Perhaps they had got the memo.

The customs official welcomed us warmly, took our passports and noticed we were born in South Africa.

'Do you have South African passports?' he asked.

'No,' we replied. We had let them lapse when we lived in Dublin and never had the need to renew.

'Do you still have family here?' he asked.

'Yes, we're going to Durban to see family and friends and then back to Cape Town to do the same.'

I felt tears as I said it. Homesickness, and sadness that I hadn't been back in time to see Mum Feely, welled up.

'Welcome back,' he said, giving me an empathetic look.

I had been holding back the longing and memories of Africa for more than 20 years. I felt homesickness like physical pain pulse through me.

'This will be the first passport stamp for Sophia and Ellie,' said Sean.

'Oh, the stamps aren't for children's passports; only for adults',' said the customs official. He gave them a wink.

'But for this special case I will make an exception.' He stamped the passports with a flourish.

'Thank you,' I said, smile wide despite my tears.

His generous spirit made Sophia and Ellie's first experience of Africa great, a place of kind heart and good humour.

We collected our bags and rolled on. We had to find the mobile-phone shop, food, our next flight, and deodorant –the effects of almost 24 hours of transit were becoming obvious. At the phone shop the counter staff were inundated with clients, some super agitated. The staff kept their cool, their good humour eventually getting the better of grumpy travellers. It was time to get on to African time and chill.

Phone in hand, we found a pharmacy. I waited with the suitcases while Sean went in with Sophia and Ellie. I was daydreaming when my attention was brought back to the moment by Sean approaching the counter with sinister-looking canisters.

'No antiperspirant!' I shouted. 'Breast cancer in a can.'

Sean lifted his eyebrows and went back to the shelf. A few minutes later he exited the pharmacy.

'You had better go and look. I can't find any that aren't antiperspirant.'

Inside, I scanned rows and rows of deodorant, and, like Sean, found only antiperspirant. I asked one of the sales ladies and she looked perplexed. We combed the shelves and eventually found a roll-on for women that didn't contain antiperspirant. We bought one for us girls, and Sean risked a canister of powerful antiperspirant deodorant for men. For someone who wouldn't let us use any cosmetics in the house and absolutely no perfume, it was a strange but necessary about-turn.

He sprayed himself liberally then sneezed.

Sophia approached and took a deep sniff.

'Hmmm,' she said. 'The *true* scent of a man.'

We all laughed. It was the tag line for the deodorant Sean had bought.

It felt good to be on holiday. The stress and responsibility of our everyday reality fell away like weights off my shoulders. As we passed out of the international section of the airport a human-size sign announced, *Welcome to the Mother City*. A tsunami of missing this place – my original homeland, its familiar words, and people – overwhelmed me. I sat on my suitcase and cried, the tears flooding out of me like a waterfall.

A few hours later we were in KwaZulu-Natal. We visited friends at their beach shack for a couple of days then went to Dad Feely in Howick. It was my first visit to the house that he and Mum had built after selling the family home where I got to know the Feelys almost three decades before.

We reveled in being together. We visited Mum Feely's place, where her ashes were spread, a river near Howick, surrounded by fields and nature. Dad and Sean cleared the protea planted in her memory and Sophia and Ellie combed the river and surrounds to pick up litter. We sat on a rock listening to the murmur of the water and felt at peace.

We planted herbs – parsley, rosemary, thyme – and celery in Dad Feely's garden. Our brief escape to a game farm was a precious shared moment and a riot of buck – impala with red hides against green scrub, kudu with twisted horns reaching to the sky, gemsbok, blesbok, waterbuck, hartebeesbok, duiker, steenbok, blue wildebeest, black wildebeest, eland - and four of the big five - lion, rhino, elephant, and buffalo. Sophia and Ellie were outgoing, more willing to take risks. We canoed a river and flew down zip lines strung across the largest indigenous forest in KwaZulu-Natal.

We left for Cape Town resolved to get back to see Dad Feely more often.

'Your South African accent is much stronger here,' said Sophia.

'That's funny. Everyone keeps asking "so where are you guys from?" as if we're foreigners,' I said.

We were on our way to visit two biodynamic vineyards. A trip to a winegrowing area was an opportunity to research ideas for our farm.

Waterkloof wine estate's glass-fronted restaurant was suspended over their winery and vine-covered hillsides, looking on to a panorama of mountains and sea. The visual extravaganza coupled with delicious food and wine created a sublime experience. I took notes and photos. Everything they were doing, from their horses in the vineyard to their winemaking facilities and restaurant were inspirational. It was 100 hectares and powered by a significant workforce and investment, in many ways a world away from our small farm in France. Their Circumstance Sauvignon Blanc was the closest we had ever tasted to our pure Sauvignon Blanc *Sincérité,* despite very different soil - granite and sandstone versus our limestone and flint stone. I put it down to our shared organic and biodynamic practices.

Our next visit was to Reyneke estate, between Somerset West and Stellenbosch, minutes from where Sean's grandparents' wine farm, that had been sold decades before, was. Johan Reyneke was a wiry, tanned surfer and farmer. After introductions in the tasting room, chat came easily.

'You know, when I was studying philosophy at Stellenbosch I couldn't get a job at a local restaurant because of my dreadlocks, so I got a job as a vineyard labourer instead,' said Johan. 'That's how I started. But let's go for a walk and look at the cows rather than just talking. I almost love them more than the vines now.'

We stepped outside.

'Look at that.' Johan pointed to a window lying on the grass in front of the building. 'I had a group of visitors this morning. One lady asked if she could let some air in and *pow*! She pushed the whole window out. I've never seen anything like it.' He laughed.

A monster dog came loping up and Johan took the cue.

'A word of warning. He has big chops and he's a farm dog. He slobbers, and it's not just saliva – it's saliva and chicken shit, and cowpat, and a bit of hay thrown in. So watch out. Also, girls,' he said to Sophia and Ellie, who were stroking him, missing their animals at home. 'Just be careful with him. We never had a problem but last week we had a lady that said she was a dog whisperer and she tried that on him, and he went nuts.'

He laughed again – an easy, relaxed laugh – then led us down a dusty red track towards the *kraal*, the Afrikaans word for a cattle enclosure.

'There they come. You see the dust cloud? That's the cows coming in for their sweets. They've had a day of eating tough boring grass; now they'll come and eat some of the post-pressing leftover grapes. They love it. It's like candy after dinner.'

The view across the vineyards to the mountains of Stellenbosch changed colour as we walked, the sky progressing from bright blue to cornflower as the sun dropped lower in the sky.

'When I started farming, we farmed with chemicals like everyone said you should. But using weedkiller and pesticides on your back in a backpack is not pleasant. So, I decided we would stop using them. But it was bad. We had all the bugs and disease that you can imagine in our vines.'

'That was our experience too,' I said. 'The first two years of organic conversion were hell – I call it "the valley of despair".'

'Just so. *Jislaaik.* Anyway, luckily, I got talking to a lady in Wellington that was doing biodynamics. I tried the solutions she proposed, and they worked.'

'That's exactly how we started biodynamics,' I said. 'We needed to solve our downy mildew problem. The organic solutions alone weren't working. Biodynamics helped us solve a practical problem. Then we found it brought so much more. It impacts every part of our life, not just our farming.'

'Yes, it's about the balance. You see the vineyard over there?' Johan pointed to the opposite hillside. 'The one that's red? It's a vineyard attacked by the leaf-roll virus; a sickness spread by the mielie bug.'

'Aphid?' I asked.

'Yes, exactly,' he replied.

'That sounds like it's transmitted in a similar way to the *flavescence dorée* virus we have in France,' said Sean. 'We saw a lot of the leaf-roll virus in Franschhoek a few days ago.'

'Yes, it's a real problem in the Cape. But you know it's all about the balance. So, like I said, we used to weedkill all the stuff on the ground but in fact this aphid prefers dandelions to vines so if we leave the weeds there's no more leaf-roll virus. Of course, we have to control the weeds, or our vineyard would be a wilderness. Those sick vineyards aren't ours by the way.' Johan laughed. He sounded like me when I disowned the chemically farmed vineyards below us.

'Anyway,' continued Johan, 'for me vine-growing is about fertilising the soil, controlling the weeds, managing the insects and pests, and preventing disease.'

I felt a smile breaking out at how similar our discourses on the vineyard were.

'So, when it comes to the fertiliser part, we used to spend about ten thousand euro a year on fertiliser; now we don't spend a cent. We have our cows instead and they generate income for us too. In the low period of the year the sale of an ox or two fills the gap. We use their dung, our wine waste, and grass from old, thatched roofs, to make our compost – you can see the heaps over there.' He pointed across the cattle pasture. 'We feed the soil in autumn with the compost, spreading it by hand. Then in late spring we bring the ducks into the vineyard to eat the pests. To attract the ducks, we place a small dose of compost next to each vine. The ducks don't eat vines but they do eat grapes, so we have to watch out. To break down heavy kitchen waste we use Australian red wrigglers in old vine barrels. We have researchers coming to study us now. The life in our soil isn't twenty percent better than the chemical farmers'; it's nine hundred percent. That's not my estimate by the way – that's what a recent group of academics found.'

He was passionate about his farm and proud that his tenacity had paid off.

'How many cows?' I asked.

'About forty at the moment for thirty-seven hectares.'

As I noted Johan's numbers, I felt a drop on my foot. I looked down. The chop monster was standing over me, gobs of sticky saliva drooling off his massive lips. I stepped back.

'For me it's about good farming. I try to get the balance. It's a tussle between building the soil and getting yield. One year I might farm for yield because I need it but then the following year I need to give back to the soil to bring back the balance,' said Johan. 'We'll check in on the winery on our way to the tasting room.'

The track hugged a vineyard full of bright-green happiness and verve, very different to some of the chemically farmed conventional vines we had seen. Johan waved to a crew member sporting a Vine Hugger T-shirt.

'There used to be pressure between the picking team and the processing team. For the pickers it's all about speed and for the processors it's about precision. So, we bought two refrigerated containers. Now when the fruit is picked, we stack it in there and it waits. No problem. The guys can take as long as they need. Let's go and taste some wine.'

Back in the whitewashed room Johan poured samples of his Sauvignon Blanc.

'Johan, may I have a wine list so I can track the wines we taste?' I asked.

'Sure,' he replied. 'If I can find one. I don't often do the tastings these days.'

As he turned the back of his neck was like leather; it was clear he spent his days out there and not in here.

'Our wines are cheap,' he said.

'Never say "cheap"!' I said. 'They're great value.'

'Cheap. Too cheap. *Jislaaik! Lekker!*' he said, laughing and looking at the wine list before handing it over to me. 'The prices have changed again! They've gone up since yesterday. Soon they won't be cheap any more. Yeeeow. The Cabernet is eight hundred rand. I've never seen that wine or tasted it!' He was laughing hard.

'Good marketing,' said Sean. 'Sounds like something Caro would do.'

We all laughed; he was joking and so was Sean.

'What's this logo that I've seen on wine bottles in SA?' I asked, pointing to a sticker of a sugarbird on a protea that was placed over the screw cap.

'That's the biodiversity and wine initiative. It's a voluntary programme to promote conservation-minded farming practices that protect nature. The seal above it is Sustainable Wine South Africa – it's the guarantee of IPW, Integrated Production of Wine. IPW is a "sustainability" label, a small step. You can still use herbicide, but you have to think about it and lower your dose. It's not ideal but it's a start. It gets people who aren't organic thinking about their chemical usage. Each year they tighten the rules. Slowly, slowly, catchy monkey.'

'It sounds like *lutte raisonnée*, the reasoned fight, and the *Haute Valeur Environnementale* or 'High Environmental Value', we have in France,' I said. 'I don't like it because it's confusing for the consumer. The lovely HVE label makes them think it's organic when it's not; it can still be packed with pesticide residues. But I see what you mean. It's helping move those that might not have made an effort on ecology otherwise.'

'Yes, and of course all this certification is expensive. Demeter biodynamic certification want two percent of our turnover to use their logo on our labels, so we don't except for our top reserve wines. We do the South African organic CERES label then we do the EU organic label and even though there's reciprocity between the EU and the US on the organic standards we have to do it again for the US. It's so expensive.'

'We know. And it's crazy that those of us not using poisons have to pay the certification fees when it should be the ones polluting who have to pay,' I said.

'Just so,' said Johan. 'Now, I have a story for you. But first, something about this Sauvignon Blanc. It's wild yeast, barrel fermented, simple.'

I caught Sean's eye, and we shared a smile at the word 'simple' that reminded us both of a hail-spattered afternoon in our tasting room that felt like aeons ago.

'No filtration, just a rock stopper to make sure the odd pair of forgotten secateurs doesn't get through,' continued Johan. 'So anyway, back to my story. A lady solicitor from Amsterdam drove her car all the way down through Africa to Cape Town. She volunteered here for a while. She said to me, "Always employ people smarter than yourself otherwise you limit your business to the level of your ability." I took that as good advice rather than a slight on my intelligence and followed what she said.'

He waited for our laughter to subside.

'I have a great team. I once sent the wrong wine to Holland. Daniel, who manages our orders now, has never made a mistake like that.'

Johan poured his Syrah. It was gorgeous, smoky, sultry, dark fruit and liquorice with a hint of *fynbos* - wild herbal scrubland unique to South Africa.

'When we started the farm, we did it with the team that had laboured with me in the vineyards when I was a student. My degree in philosophy taught me that empowering people meant giving them the "capability to choose" – it's more about that than about Maslow's hierarchy of needs. Regardless of whether these needs are met or not, we're only happy when we have choice. So, I asked the guys what they wanted. I gave them choice. They said they wanted houses and education, so we went all out for that. We still offer university education to all our staff and children, but you have to stay ten years with the company to get a house. We burnt our fingers with people leaving after a year and selling the house.'

He poured Reyneke Cornerstone red. It was red fruit and bright, full of flavour.

'Anyway, back to the idea of choice and team. We know that the team is the cornerstone of our business hence the name of this wine to reflect that and our choice to offer choice to our people, especially education. So, one of the original team who started with us is now our gardener; he's illiterate but his daughter Lizaan has a university degree and she runs the place. She's the one who has set the new prices and the price for the new Cabernet Sauvignon. With her in charge soon the wines won't be cheap, but they will still be great value.' He caught my eye and we laughed.

'Back at the start I was sitting in this room, the place where we used to milk our cows. Things were really tough. We had bought houses for our staff, but the wine business was rough. We were close to closing the doors. I really didn't know what to do. Then a lady walked in here and tasted our wines. She said she was from CNN and she wanted to buy all our wine for a big international event in Johannesburg. She followed through and I flew up for the event. Next thing I was being introduced to Madiba. Now, you know, it isn't good me being white, Afrikaans and a farmer given the history of South Africa, but President Mandela started a conversation smooth and in his stride, saying in Afrikaans, 'So how is it going with our farmers?' What an experience meeting him. But it also turned us around. From the precipice that lucky break in 2002 took us from strength to strength. We had already changed to farming without chemicals. We started the natural farming in 1999 but only started the biodynamic certification in 2006. At the start we had four families depending on the farm; now we have sixteen.'

'Impressive,' I said. In my mind I calculated, compared our ten hectares with one full-time worker, Sean, to his, around four times our size with 16 people. They could hand-weed, hand-spray and have enough people in the winery for it to be relatively peaceful at harvest time. The minimum wage in South Africa at the time meant that almost two days of work cost the same as one hour in France.

'It's intense right now, harvest time. I'm looking forward to going to the beach and surfing, not thinking, when it's finished,' said Johan.

'We know that feeling,' I said. 'Maybe we need to take up surfing.'

'For me it's important to make good wine but also to enjoy my life,' said Johan.

As we took off back to Cape Town, I reflected that we would benefit from remembering his philosophy. Our holiday offered a chance to do that. In Cape Town Aunt Sally, who visited for my parents' golden wedding anniversary, organised a big family party. We talked, laughed, ate, and played the racing demons. Intergenerational family contact felt comforting. Despite having been away for so long, I felt a sense of belonging. The trip to South Africa reminded me how much we missed having time to relax, to be with friends and family – things we had sacrificed for ten years in order to turn our business around.

CHAPTER 17

Seeking Equilibrium

When we returned home the daffodils were out but there was still a bite in the air. Our trip to South Africa had been a welcome break but things were not perfect between us, and we both knew we had to find a better balance between our work and our personal life.

Sean and I were doing maintenance, cleaning and treating the tasting-room and Lodge decks with natural oil. The night before Sean had insulted my dinner again and I had cracked. We got into a roaring fight that left me and our daughters crying. I found myself wondering if this was the man I had fallen in love with so many years before.

'We have to stop fighting in front of the kids,' said Sean. 'They went to sleep after midnight they were so upset.'

'Then you should hold back before criticising my cooking,' I said. 'What's wrong? You seem so dissatisfied. We're no better than business partners. We have to change or call it quits.'

'That's the second time you've said you want a divorce,' he said.

'What?' I said.

'Yes, that's the second time you've said we have to call it quits,' said Sean. 'What do you expect me to do? Is that what you really want?'

I looked into his eyes for what felt like the first time in years and was mute for a few moments. He was right. I had said it twice. We had grown so far apart that for a second, I saw that as an option. In that moment of consideration, I felt like I had been hit by a wrecking ball; I saw our lives transformed, torn apart, as if my very being was split in two. Deep down I knew it was not the right choice for me or for anyone in our family. Then I felt a deep tenderness for this man I loved. I had been a bad-tempered menopausal monster. That momentary flicker of 'go' was my ego speaking.

When we let our spirits speak, we were on another level. We hadn't given them time to be together. Our egos were in charge. We had been going so hard to build our business that our spirits had taken off in opposite directions. We had to find our connection again.

'No,' I said, feeling shocked as I realised exactly what I had been threatening.

'Neither do I, Caro. I love you. I want to stay together but I can't take this constant questioning.'

Sean's eyes filled with tears, and I felt mine do the same. It was our first real conversation in ages – and it wasn't about labels, corks, or sulphites.

'I don't want to keep doing the hard physical graft I do every day for another ten years,' said Sean, ignoring my comment about cooking criticism and restating what he had said when we were blending. 'My body is telling me to slow down. I love being in the garden, growing things, tending the vines, and I don't mind that physical work, but when it comes to pipe-work and barrel-work in the winery I've had enough.'

'But we've just turned the corner: the wines are virtually selling themselves; we know the ropes; everything is rolling a bit easier. With the investments over the last few years our cash flow going forward will be better. People love our wines and tours; the business is growing. We'd be mad to walk away. You're so good at winemaking. Look at the positive comments we get about our wines.'

'I want a simpler life,' said Sean. 'Remember, when we came here, it was to live a more self-sufficient life, to get away from the rat race. I feel like we're under more pressure now than we were then. The business is getting bigger and more complex all the time. I want to be more self-sufficient and have less administration, bureaucracy, and stress.'

'But we have to grow to afford a full-time person. Think of all the projects we'd like to tackle: sheep and cheese, a biodynamic display garden, permaculture, more education, tourism and food pairing.'

I had been coasting along thinking we were into the 'plain sailing' in the life cycle of our business. We had offered Cécile a role with us once her apprenticeship was complete. She was going travelling for six months and we hoped would return after her trip. Sean's confessions were a swift reminder that there are no certainties in life or in business. Our fights were an explosive combination of my menopause and of Sean feeling unhappy, but perhaps there was an element of Johan Reyneke's philosophy of choice in our behaviour too. After what we had put in and considering how far we were into our vineyard dream, it felt like we didn't have any choice but to continue. We had lost our freedom.

We finished the deck and started collecting up our tools.

'We won't solve this now,' said Sean. 'I'm just saying we need to consider our long-term well-being.'

We agreed that we needed to talk more.

I raced up to Saussignac to fetch Ellie. The sun was out at last after a slow start to spring. The weather was too good to waste inside so Ellie and I decided to go for a knock on the Saussignac tennis court after she had finished her *goûter*. She and Sophia had started tennis lessons two years before.

We walked up with the racquets. Saussignac village was winter quiet; no one except a few pigeons. The bell tower rang, echoing through the square and the leafless trees.

We started with warm-up races bouncing a ball across the court. That always generated a laugh and did us good but when we started knocking Ellie wasn't playing well. She got mad. The madder she got the worse she played, and the worse she played, the madder she got. It was an infernal circle, and she became totally unpleasant, showing me an excellent example of what the French call *fait la tête*, 'to be in a bad mood'.

'We need to get back. Papa said we had to be home at quarter to seven at the latest,' I said. 'I'll collect the balls outside the court then we must go.'

As I did that, Ellie served a few good balls, but she was still in a foul temper. I walked ahead to give her time to cool down, then waited near Saussignac Castle for her to catch up.

'You know, Ellie, one of the most important things about sport is to be a 'good sport'. That means being nice when you lose and keeping a happy face even when you're not happy with how you're playing,' I said.

'Hurumph,' responded Ellie.

'I know how you feel. I used to get really mad when I lost and believed that I should have won, that I could play better than I had,' I said.

'Hmmm,' said Ellie. She lifted her head and looked me in the eye for the first time since she had got into her temper.

'And getting mad doesn't help you play better, does it? In fact, it makes you play worse,' I said.

Ellie nodded.

'So next time just relax and try to enjoy playing even if you aren't playing your best. You need to be Zen if you want to play well.'

She seemed to have taken in what I said.

We reached our front door and Sean opened it from inside, his left hand held high in the air. It was wrapped in white tape that had ominous red smudges on it.

'Don't worry, it's just a little cut. Nothing to get excited about,' he said, backing away into the kitchen. 'I've cleaned it out, run it under loads of clear water, put Betadine on and taped it up. No need to panic.'

I dropped the tennis bag and opened the cupboard to grab the car keys.

'You could just re-tape it with surgical tape,' said Sean. 'We don't even have to go to the clinic. It's just a little cut.'

Sophia was behind him, wide-eyed and shaking her head.

'We're going to the hospital,' I said. 'Have you got your *carte vitale* and your phone? Girls, get yourselves some dinner and get ready for bed.'

'I'll make fried eggs,' said Sophia.

'No. I don't want you using the flame while we're out, especially with a crisis already on the go.'

'This isn't a crisis,' said Sean. 'It's just a little cut.'

It was *déjà vu* to ten years before, when Sean cut off a third of his finger on the same hand and I had raced him to Bergerac hospital. This time we knew that Sainte-Foy-la-Grande was slightly closer and for a cut like this would probably be faster.

In a quarter of an hour, we were at the hospital. I pressed the buzzer on the intercom in the waiting room and within minutes Sean had been whisked behind the plasterboard walls and I was left alone.

A petite blonde woman and her young son came in. Her husband had a crushed foot, a work accident that had happened half an hour before. He was already behind the plasterboard walls. His boss had brought him in, and she had just arrived, hoping she could take him home.

We sat on hard metal chairs. The small room had a coffee and soup vending machine, a few posters about hygiene, an empty table, and the intercom. There was not a single magazine or book. The wait stretched out ahead of us. With each set of footsteps or voice on the other side of the door, I felt a flicker of hope that died as they disappeared again.

Half an hour. One hour. My partner in impatience organised for a friend to fetch her son and give him dinner. I got up and did some stretches.

'I'm so hungry,' she said. She rose and bought a cup of soup from the machine that had been humming intermittently at my side.

About 20 minutes later, I succumbed and bought a 50-cent tomato soup from the machine too. It was horrible but I was desperate. I hadn't thought to drink water after tennis, and there was no sign of a water fountain.

At one and a half hours, I got up and did more stretches. If I ever returned, I would bring a book and a snack pack.

At two hours, I decided to go home and come back when he was ready.

I rang the intercom.

'It's Madame Feely, the wife of the man who cut his hand.'

'He's arriving,' said the nurse.

After another 15 minutes, my partner in impatience said, 'Well, he's arriving sometime tonight.'

We both laughed hard, the humour easing our worry.

'I hear a voice. I think it's my husband,' she said.

The door opened. It was Sean. She and I laughed again, and Sean looked at me quizzically, his left hand bandaged thick and held up like he was giving us a very large one-finger salute.

'Ah, bad luck for me,' said the blonde.

'I hope it isn't too long,' I said. 'Good luck to your husband for a fast recovery.'

'Thank you, and to you too,' she replied.

I held the door open for Sean. He passed through and we walked to the car.

'How many stitches?' I asked.

'Seven.'

I guffawed. "'Just a little cut, nothing to worry about. We could just tape it closed.'"

'I don't think he really needed to put the last one in,' said Sean defensively.

I laughed even harder; a little from euphoria that Sean was OK and a little from the absurdity of his comments.

'Still, as a way of getting out of doing the winemaking it's going a bit far,' I said.

Sean smiled.

He had finished all the winemaking steps that were required before bottling otherwise I would have been back in there like I was in our first year. I thanked my lucky stars. I wouldn't know which end of a barrel was up after years of Sean doing all of that part of the business on his own.

Then we were home. The girls had shared a jar of organic baked beans for supper. Sean went to lock up the chickens with Ellie helping since he only had one hand. Sophia let her friends know the latest in the drama via social media. It was way past their bedtime but on nights like this that would go down in family memory that didn't matter.

I decided to cook fried eggs, comfort food. Our chickens were well settled, and we were back to enjoying the self-sufficiency they added to our lives. Sheep were still a way off.

I placed the eggs on rough slices of organic bread next to purslane and chicory – two salads that had made it through winter, with a dressing of local sunflower oil and cider vinegar. The bread, made from heritage wheat grown by an organic farmer up the road, was a find by Cécile that had become a favourite with guests on our tours. It was nutty and satisfying, a world away from industrial bread.

We lifted our glasses and did cheers in the family way.

'To health,' I said.

'To health' echoed round the table.

'My friend Lauren's mum had a heart palpitation in her sleep,' said Sophia, following that train of thought. 'She could have died. She nearly died before when she had cancer on her kidneys. That's when you realise the most important thing is your health.'

'You are so right, Sophia,' I said.

'So, when people complain that organic is too expensive, they only need to think about that. Once you have cancer it's too late,' she added.

I could not have said it better myself.

'That egg is so good,' said Sean.

'A feast. So simple and such flavour,' I added.

'Well done for keeping calm, Sophia,' said Sean. 'You were so cool in the crisis.'

'I thought you said it wasn't a crisis?' I said.

We all laughed.

'When I came in, I thought Papa was going to ask me to wash beetroot – the basin in the sink was so full of red,' said Sophia.

I pictured it, and it took me back to when Sean slashed his arm on the vine trimmer, another accident that happened in our first year. There was so much blood trailed through the kitchen, and in the sink, that I kept having to sit down and put my head between my legs to stop myself from fainting.

'And well done to both of you for having your supper and getting ready for bed,' I said.

'And well done, Mum, for not having a TSA,' said Sophia.

TSA was her latest saying, as in 'Total Stress Attack' – what mums did when their kids forgot their school bag and they were already at the bus stop or when their husband chopped off his finger.

⋙ ⋘

Aideen and Barry, our friends from Dublin, arrived for their Easter holiday that coincided with helping with our annual bottling. With bottling complete, they moved my office out to the tasting room. It felt like freedom, like when I took my duvet cover back from the Cottage. Moving the office out of our living space to the business area gave us back a little of our personal life; part of finding balance. I bought an office chair, one that had proper back support, to replace the old wicker chair that had travelled the world with us.

Menopause had been akin to the phase of conversion to organic that I called the 'valley of despair'. When we started the organic conversion and stopped the chemicals it was like 'cold turkey' for the vines. They were weak and susceptible; the mycorrhizae had not had time to build in the soil and their immunity was weak. It took three years for them to make the transition. I was into my third year of transition, and I was approaching the other side: my hormonal balance was coming back. My dreams about dying had stopped. My periods had stopped. I was close to, if not at, the other side.

Sophia and Ellie announced that they had sleepovers with friends and would both be out the same evening.

'Date night for us then?' I said to Sean.

Despite our best intentions, the last time we had had a date night was on the truffling weekend almost four years before.

'Maybe,' said Sean.

Spring had been cold and wet, but the day dawned with bright sunshine and a fresh breeze. We packed our daughters off to the respective friends.

'So should we go out?' I asked.

'No, let's stay in,' said Sean. 'I picked up our organic beef box and I have two steaks in the fridge. If you do the starter, I'll do the main.'

'Deal,' I said.

I set a table for two with tablecloth, napkins, and candles, angled to take advantage of the view from the *salon* that looked onto Feely vineyards and a patchwork of farmland and plum blossoms in the valley below. The setting and table looked idyllic and romantic. Satisfied with my decorative efforts, I returned to the kitchen where Sean had music playing and cooking preparations under way.

While I made herbed goat's cheese toasts for our starter, Sean's knife flashed through spinach and onions fresh from the garden. We found the music of Sophie B. Hawkins online, an album we had fallen in love to decades before. Her erotic lyrics were backed by smoky rock, perfect music for a date night. 'California, Here I Come' started playing as I poured glasses of Sauvignon Blanc, a Californian biodynamic wine made under the advice of Philippe Coderey, a friend met in Santa Cruz. He had passed by to visit a couple of months before bearing it as a gift. It was delicious, balanced with good acidity and a roundness we didn't usually find on Sauvignon Blanc in France.

With wine and goat's cheese in hand, we chatted, looking intermittently on to the view and into each other's eyes. Our conversation flowed through current affairs, new adventures, dreams.

Sean served the organic steak pan-fried to perfection with a side of homegrown spinach and beans, and I poured us each a glass of our no-sulphites-added *Grâce* red wine. We soaked in the moment, the exceptional food, the view on to the vineyard and Sean's bountiful *potager*, the music.

I felt like scales had been lifted off my eyes, like I was seeing Sean clearly for the first time in ages. He was still the man I had fallen in love with. We chatted into the night, candles burning low and lights twinkling in the valley, enjoying each other's company like we had when we first fell in love. After being missing for most of the perimenopause and menopause, my libido returned. The valley of despair was officially over – perhaps Sean had slipped a little truffle aphrodisiac into the sauce.

I could see why so many long relationships broke up around this point. Menopause was a tough transition. We had to keep reinventing ourselves to keep us and our relationship strong. Sean was the love of my life, the only shoe that fit. I could not imagine growing out of him, but it was frightening how close we had come to tearing apart. We had so much shared history, so much shared happiness together, a family, a life.

Each morning I rose at 5.45 a.m., went downstairs, and did two salutations to the sun and Five Tibetans. Sean was usually up with the dawn with me, out doing handwork in the vineyard and the *potager* before the heat of the day. We kissed each other hello instead of passing like two strangers. After our greeting I took my tea and crossed the courtyard, the crunch of the gravel under my feet, my eyes turned heavenwards to marvel at the sky. Earlier in the spring the brilliance of the stars was exceptional; I saw formations and clusters I had never noticed before.

As the days grew longer, I watched the ever-changing sunrise and Sean's evolving garden and vines in a different light every day. We debated options long and hard. We weren't earning what we could have in the city, but we were stewards of the land; we were taking care of a small part of the earth, and each year we saw progress that filled us with hope and joy.

Like any work there were days where we felt down, like it was an uphill battle, but we were making a difference to this earth where we had rooted and to the people that came in contact with our passion for organic wine and organic farming. Our plans were evolving; we were looking at ways to increase our self-sufficiency and at equipment that would ease Sean's work in the winery. Sophia started giving Sean lessons to improve his French grammar. The inspirational vineyards we had seen in South Africa sparked new ideas for our vineyard and wine tourism. I wanted to share our passion for organic beyond our farm gate and to do more writing. With intense debate we were working out what we wanted to do. We hadn't found the perfect balance yet but we felt renewed energy for what we were doing and we had reignited our passion for each other. I had a feeling our vineyard adventures were far from over.

Message from Caro

Thank you for buying this book. Reading it, you will have realised that I am passionate about organic and how critical it is to support organic and local food. Each of us can make change happen. We don't have time to wait for governments to legislate it. We can do it ourselves by making informed choices every day. If no one buys chemically grown food farmers will stop using systemic pesticides and change to organic practices.

Over the coming years, I wish to share my passion beyond our farm, to do more outreach, more book festivals and book tours. If you would like me to chat with your book club online or if you wish to host a local event, please get in touch at caro@carofeely.com.

I also invite you to join my mailing list at www.carofeely.com and follow me at https://www.instagram.com/carofeely/ where I regularly share information about farming, ecology and how we can make a difference.

You can find out more about my books at www.carofeely.com, about Feely certified organic vineyard, yoga and accommodation at www.chateaufeely.com and the walking tours, wine tours and wine school at www.frenchwineadventures.com.

I look forward to seeing you online, in the Dordogne or beyond. Thank you for joining me on this journey.

With very best wishes, Caro

Acknowledgments

A memoir is a personal journey, a way of making sense of the past, so my biggest thank you goes to my family, Sean, Sophia and Ellie, for their participation in this adventure and for supporting me in sharing these intimate portraits of our lives – from my perspective bien sûr. Sean says I write great fiction.

Thank you to our family: my mum and dad, Cliff and Lyn Wardle; Dad Feely; the Bristow family; my sister Jacquie and brother Garth. Thank you also to the friends that are part of this story: Thierry and Isabelle Daulhiac, Pierre and Laurence de St Viance, Antoine Mariau, Dave and Amanda Moore, Ian, Brigit and Chiara Wilson, Chris and Dave Drake, Fearn and Andrea King, and Cécile Rousseau.

Last but not least, thank you to my readers for reading my books. A special thank you to readers who have written to me over the years – your emails and letters have provided great motivation to keep writing.

Grape Expectations

A Family's Vineyard Adventure in France

Book 1 of The Vineyard Series.

What does it take to follow your dreams?

The wine filled my mouth with plum and blackberry sensations. A picture of a vineyard drenched in sunlight formed in my mind. Sean drew me rudely back to our small suburban home.

'How can they be in liquidation if they make wine this good?'

When Caro and Sean find the perfect vineyard near Bordeaux their dreams of a new life in France are about to come true. They arrive, with a toddler and a newborn, to face a dilapidated farmhouse, and challenges including accidents with agricultural equipment, cultural misunderstandings, and money worries. Undeterred, they embark on the biggest adventure of their lives – learning to make wine from the roots up.

Reviews

'A beautifully written tale of passion and guts.' Alice Feiring, Author

'Captivating reading' Destination France

'An inspiring story of how one couple changed their lives.' Jamie Ivey, Author

'I was delighted by this book, by what it says about the passion of winemaking, France, family life, and the challenges that build a marriage.' Martin Walker, bestselling author of the Bruno, Chief of Police series

E-book ISBN: 978-2-9586304-1-6
Print Book ISBN: 978-2-9586304-0-9
By Caro Feely

Saving Our Skins

BUILDING A VINEYARD
DREAM IN FRANCE

Sequel to Grape Expectations. Book 2 of The Vineyard
Series.

'Earnest and winning... sincere and passionate'
The New York Times

'We have to get to the next level, or we have to get out,' I
said.
'We have to have more vines and more accommodation,'
replied Sean.
Both would take investment we didn't have.

For Caro and Sean, building their vineyard dream and
overcoming challenges that include a devastating frost,
bureaucracy, and renovation setbacks, will take courage,
ingenuity, and luck.

This book is about love and taking risks while transforming a piece of land into a flourishing organic vineyard and making a new life in France. It explores the reality of following your dream, challenges of building a new business, renovating in France and raising a family as a working mum; and includes nature, delicious food and wine, and voyages to Napa and Sonoma wine regions in the USA, and to Alsace, Bergerac, Bordeaux, and Burgundy wine regions in France.

Reviews

'So impassioned that it could inspire you to drop all security, move to the backwaters of France, and bet your life, all for the love of making wine.' Alice Feiring, author and wine writer

E-book ISBN: 978-2-9586304-3-0
Print book ISBN: 978-2-9586304-2-3
By Caro Feely
First published in 2014.

Cultivating Change

REGENERATING LAND AND LOVE IN THE AGE OF CLIMATE CRISIS

What will it take to change? Can we resuscitate our relationship with the earth? And with each other?

Cultivating Change follows the emotional journey of Caro and Sean as they regenerate their vineyard in France and rewrite their love story in the face of climate change. The book explores family dynamics, work life balance, yoga, organic farming, food, and personal awakening.

Join Caro as she searches for wisdom to address the climate crisis and to breathe new life into a stumbling marriage in this powerful new memoir.

Key themes: Primary themes: Climate change, Marriage, Wine, Vineyards, Organic farming, Regenerative farming, Biodiversity, Yoga, Personal awakening.

Secondary themes: Seasonal Affective Disorder (SAD), Raising teenagers as a working mother, Transitioning to the empty nest, Gastronomy, Voyages in France, Ireland, Italy, Japan, South Africa, and the United Kingdom.

Reviews

'Powerful and inspiring' Jacqui Brown, Book blogger

'A must read. Passionate, challenging, and informative.' Helen Melser, Author

'A thoroughly enjoyable read and a wake-up call about how our actions affect our planet.' Tora Shand

Print book ISBN: 978-2-9586304-6-1
E-book ISBN: 978-2-9586304-7-8
By Caro Feely
Published 15 June 2023.

Saving Sophia

Neonatal surgery, blisters and bliss on the rocky road to Motherhood

"The paediatrician came back without our baby.
'I'm afraid we have a problem.'
Stars bounced around my vision of the doctor's talking head, his voice far away like a dream. I felt like I was sinking into a void and leant back to steady myself on the bed. We had experienced the deepest, most life affirming event the night before, the birth of our first child. Now she was being taken away. It was a moment that would take us on an intense journey and change the course of our lives."

'Saving Sophia' is a page-turning true-life story of pregnancy, birth, ICU, breastfeeding, first time parenting, postnatal depression, and raising a family. A gripping and humorous account of a nail-biting entry into parenting that offers a glimpse into, and a reminder of, how miraculous raising a family is.

This is a memoir with love at its heart, a story of first-time mothering, family, and friendship.

Key themes

Primary themes: motherhood, ICU baby, breastfeeding, first time parenting.

Secondary themes: healthy living, yoga, belonging, immigration, stop pesticides, stop glyphosate, postnatal depression/ postpartum depression, follow your dream.

Reviews

'I loved this wonderful book.' Julie Haigh, We Love Memoirs

'A heart-warming and deeply moving memoir of love and family.' Martin Walker, bestselling author

'A beautifully written memoir... I couldn't put it down.' Jacqui Brown, Book blogger

'What a read! Unputdownable,' Jeanne Wissing

E-book ISBN: 978-2-9586304-9-2
Print book ISBN: 978-2-9586304-8-5
By Caro Feely
Publication 5 November 2023.
A prequel to the vineyard series.

Have you enjoyed this book?

Thank you for buying this book. If you enjoyed it please consider putting a review on your favourite book review site (e.g. amazon, goodreads). Reviews make a significant difference to a book's visibility.

For free samples, advance notice of new books and more, we invite you to sign up to Caro's newsletter at www.carofeely.com .

Made in United States
North Haven, CT
21 April 2024

51607259R00178